# Resilient

# Forgiveness

Memoir by
BARBARA J. WRIGHT

TRILOGY
A WHOLLY OWNED SUBSIDIARY OF **TBN**
PROFESSIONAL PUBLISHING MEETS POWERFUL PROMOTION

*Reselient Forgiveness*

Trilogy Christian Publishers

A Wholly Owned Subsidiary of Trinity Broadcasting Network

2442 Michelle Drive, Tustin, CA 92780

For information, address Trilogy Christian Publishing

Rights Department, 2442 Michelle Drive, Tustin, CA 92780.

Trilogy Christian Publishing/ TBN and colophon are trademarks of Trinity Broadcasting Network.

For information about special discounts for bulk purchases, please contact Trilogy Christian Publishing.

10 9 8 7 6 5 4 3 2 1

Library of Congress Cataloging-in-Publication Data is available.

ISBN 979-8-89333-211-7

ISBN 979-8-89333-212-4 (ebook)

"Mother to Son"
Langston Hughes


Well, son, I'll tell you:
Life for me ain't been no crystal stair.

It's had tacks in it,
And splinters,
And boards torn up,

And places with no carpet on the floor—
Bare.

But all the time I'se been
a-climbin' on,
And reachin' landin's,
And turnin' corners,

And sometimes goin' in the dark
Where there ain't been no light.
So boy, don't you turn back.

Don't you set down on the steps'
Cause you finds it's kinder hard.
Don't you fall now—
For I'se still goin', honey, I'se still climbin',
And life for me ain't been no crystal stair.

# Table of Contents

# The Fruits of the Spirit

They are

Love,

Joy,

Peace,

Patience,

Kindness,

Goodness,

Faithfulness,

Gentleness,

and Self-Control

**This is what worked for me as a believer.**

# Foreword

I have talked about writing this book for a decade. I woke up at about four a.m. on Father's Day, thinking I needed to get chapter one started. This is ironic to me in that much of my struggles in life were at the wrath of my so-called father. But looking back at my childhood and adult life, I can see the cycles and struggles that I overcame as a blessing. My goal in this book is not just to produce a memoir and share my story, but to write a story that might serve as a guide to others about how to navigate the thickets of life.

Like all of us, I am the sum total of my experiences. For me, those experiences included love, betrayal, abandonment, poverty, and neglect. There has also been abuse—mental, emotional, and physical—which has caused me a great deal of pain. But I am unlike others. I remain uninjured by the hurt people who meant me harm. Yes, through it all, I have enjoyed the kind of success that only faith can bring.

Life, whether you are willing to accept it or not, is a struggle. But hurt people do not always become people who hurt others. Despite my struggles, I am living proof of this.

My greatest fear in actually writing this book has been where to begin. In order to be successful in this endeavor, I sought out others to write the book for me.

It was my belief that ghostwriters could write the book quicker and better than I could. But I was not successful in finding someone to do it in the timeframe it needed to be done, so I decided to do it myself. After all, no one can tell my story like I can. I've lived it. I have written it. And now I share it.

I have met and listened to many people who have survived similar nightmares. I've also met people who are still struggling with the ugly scars left by others. Whether you are experiencing abandonment, neglect, abuse, repeated rape, domestic violence, extreme poverty, or divorce, know that you are not alone. May the words in this book show you the path forward. Writing this has helped me release the pain of the past once and for all. I pray it does the same for you.

This book is to encourage, inspire, heal, and deliver individuals who may find a resemblance to themselves in my story. I know without a doubt that because I made it through, you can make it too.

I want you to have this to hold on to as you read this book: that despite the pain you've lived though, you can succeed too.

Now, let the story begin.

# *Childhood*

*"Let the redeemed of the LORD tell their story
—those he redeemed from the hand of the foe."*

Psalm 107:2 NIV

Of seven children, I was the second born of my teenage mother. I was born with fire-engine red hair. I had beautiful dimples, and I was a happy baby. It was my natural beauty, however, that first began to cause trouble for me. My pretty legs, deep dimples, and red hair were more of a curse than a blessing. At least, as far as my stepmother was concerned.

In total, my mother, Frances, had seven children: five sons and two daughters. She herself was one of thirteen children. Mom, as I call her, was born in a Delaware household where the father was the breadwinner, and Grandpop taught good, strong work ethics. He was very strict in raising his children. Grandpop had stable spiritual beliefs. He was an entrepreneur before that word became so popular. Grandpop worked as a woodsman and a waterman. My mother and her brothers and sisters stripped bark from freshly cut trees, tossing the logs onto trucks to be hauled to mills for processing. They threw pulpwood as well as fished and tongued oysters in brutally cold weather along the Atlantic shore and inland waterways.

If there was a perfect person in my life, it would have to be the stout, somewhat plump woman I called Mom-Hattie. My grandfather's first wife was ever present and loving, a woman who nurtured her family with a gentle but stern countenance. She also had wisdom. You could see it when she gently steered someone away from an emotional disaster or a bad decision. Her words were stern but caring. I never heard a cross word or even a raised voice. I like to think my personality grew from her.

My grandmother juggled many tasks. She managed the family income as a stay-at-home mother. She was also an excellent financial manager despite her education being only elementary level. Not only did my grandparents own the house where they raised their children, but they also owned acres of wooded property. This was not easy to do as a Black family during the 1930s and 1940s, but they worked together and made it happen. My grandmother and grandpop managed to provide food and shelter for extended family and friends (in addition to their own children). There was always a presence of spirituality that I adopted without realizing it.

At the innocent age of five, while living in my grandpop's house, I experienced the bitterness of sexual abuse. That first time was not the last. My grandpop's brother would appear to be the best great-uncle a child could have, but only when in front of others. He would cuddle, buy very nice things for me, give me money, and appear to genuinely love me as an innocent child. What no one knew was that he would also molest me while he was drunk. I hated him. At five years old, I was already being stripped of my dignity and my self-esteem, and I was a totally confused child. I suppose my grandmother's death was so devastating to everyone in the family that the children were not the top priority. I am not absolutely sure what was on anyone's mind; perhaps there were signs of the incest that the adults overlooked. I just know my childhood included ugly emotional scars that stayed with me for the rest of my life.

During the next thirteen years, I was bounced between my young mother and my supposedly biological father. This man was my older brother's father. He was supposed to be my father too. But as you will see, the term is applied loosely.

When my brother and I were put in the home of our father, Coley Sr., and his wife Betty, it was the beginning of our worst days. This woman became my evil stepmother, literally. My mother and this woman had many fights, some verbal and some physical. Once they were said to have fought like men in front of the church, a fist-filled blow and yelling match on a Sunday morning. Betty had been madly in love with my mother's older brother before taking up with my father, Coley Sr., and so because I was beautiful like my mother, Betty hated me. I did not stand a chance living in a house with her. My brother resembled our father with dark skin and striking body language; my stepmother did not care for Coley Jr. either. We were in for abuse, neglect, and torture for more than a decade.

For the first few years, we lived with this wicked woman and our father in extreme conditions. At the same time, my mother had a new man—with whom she had two more children. Questions often nagged at me about how we ended up so unwanted: Why couldn't I and my brother live with my mother? What did we do to deserve this? How could a woman walk away from her offspring? Did anyone really care about us?

In my stepmother's house, I remember Coley Jr. and I being too afraid to do anything wrong. Almost every day, we were falsely accused and punished with switches we had to fetch ourselves from outside. We were told the switches had to be long and pliable. We had to gather several branches that were woven together so that whippings would cause deep, stinging pain, leaving welts on our arms, thighs, backs, and even sometimes our faces. We were also pummeled with fists, belt buckles, or any blunt object within reach. As long as they generated pain and humiliation, my stepmother used it.

I remember one summer day in particular. My then-seven-year-old brother and I were left home alone. When our stepmother came home from work, she asked what we had been doing all day. We explained we had been playing.

"Liars," Betty said.

She then told me to lay on the bed on my back. She then told my brother to lay face down on top of me and show her what we had been doing. His face stopped inches from mine in the strange missionary position, and we froze. We were clueless. She continued to threaten us and told him to move up and down on top of me, implying that he and I had been having sex. When we refused, she gave us both a whipping so bad that I thought it would take a lifetime to get over. What a sick mind she had.

Later in life, I was told that she had been abused so brutally as a child that she tried to kill her father by poisoning his drink. It makes sense to me, now that I am an adult, that this was the way she decided to raise us children—children that were not her own and that she did not want. Of course, our father didn't care. I found out later from his sister that he too didn't want children. And all of our lives, my brother and I felt every bit of their hate. This feeling of being unwanted continued to follow me for most of my life. It took me many more years and experiences to understand that I don't need to be a victim anymore, even though I was victimized. In fact, it would not be until after many of my abusers were on their deathbeds that I began to see the generational cycles that I was born into but born to overcome.

# Perseverance

*"When my father and my mother forsake me,
then the Lord will take care of me."*

Psalm 27:10 NKJV

Coley Jr. and I moved to North Carolina when I was about eight years old. This was our father's birthplace and where he lived as a child. He, like our mother, was one of thirteen children. His family was loving and spiritually grounded. His mother owned farmland, growing a variety of produce and raising turkeys. While the rest of the world viewed turkeys as noble icons of the Thanksgiving holiday, I found them to be mean, tall, and dirty. At that young age, when I stood among the birds, level with the ugliest thing I'd ever looked in the eye, I had to tread carefully around turkey droppings.

My father's brother, Paul, better known as Uncle Reds, grew tobacco and cotton out in the country, although he and his girlfriend lived in town. They would drive out each day to tend the crops and, in the evening, return to town. Uncle Reds and Aunt Viola had one son, Glenn. I was always jealous of Glenn being an only child. Being the second of seven on my mom's side alone and caught in between two households was disheartening, to say the least. We all thought Glenn had an uncomplicated life as an only child with wealthy parents. However, looks are sometimes deceiving—especially for those who look like they have it made. Before my father passed, he shocked me and my cousins by telling us that Uncle Reds was not Glenn's father.

Odell, one of my father's sisters, lived with my grandmother, whom we called Grandmom Bessie. Aunt Odell was heavyset. One of her eyes was set awkwardly, always staring slightly away from the target. She claimed to be a God-fearing woman, which I always thought was ironic, considering she had seven children and not all had the same father. I guess everyone has their own path to God. The last two of her children were sired by Robbie, her crazy boyfriend who rode a bicycle everywhere he went, a foot-long machete mounted across the handlebars. Since he was a heavy drinker, his appearance invoked fear in anyone he encountered. He and Aunt Odell bickered constantly. She was always chastising her children, using switches to reinforce the discipline. Aunt Odell's seven children were Alphonzo, Bessie, Betty Joyce, Willie Dee, Jessie (known as JT), Ruby Jean, and James. James was the wild character of the bunch. From the age of nine, he dipped snuff and cursed out anyone at any time. Young or old, it didn't matter to James.

Grandmom Bessie was very kind to me and my brother and always tried to protect us from the cruelty we experienced from Betty and Coley Sr. I used to walk past her room, hearing her talking to God, knowing that her prayers always reached His listening ears.

In addition to Aunt Odell, my father's other sister was Aunt Estelle, known as Aunt Doll. She was sweet and kind and was married to Uncle Shugg. They were a cute, short little couple who lived a few miles from the family farm. They had three daughters: Lois Ann, who always reminded us younger cousins that she was the oldest; Patricia Ann, who was about my age and one of my playmates; and Wanda Faye.

Aunt Doll's family lived in a small home located down a long lane off the main road. She had a ready smile but worked hard in the fields. Aunt Doll closed her curtains every night with clothespins. She addressed everybody as "sugar" in a soft-spoken voice. Her children knew she was serious and meant business when she called them by both their names: Tricia Ann, Lois Ann, or Wanda Faye.

Uncle Shugg smiled all the time, and Aunt Doll always made sure we had plenty to eat, beginning with a breakfast of hot scratch biscuits and plastic buckets filled with bacon pieces that adorned scrambled eggs. Working in the field didn't pay well, but it paid enough to feed Aunt Doll and her husband as well as their family. Her husband also did farm work, so in the mornings, she would make a pan of homemade biscuits, and there would be a bucket of bacon pieces and ham slices that she would attempt to cook if there was enough time before the bus was scheduled to arrive.

She was a kind and generous woman and was quick to speak against our stepmother's maltreatment of my brother and me whenever she caught wind of it. My father and Betty, however, ignored Aunt Doll. Somehow we lived with all of this turmoil during our one-year-long stay in Wilson, and Aunt Doll's care for us was certainly a bright spot in our early years. So too was Aunt Mabelle's cooking.

Aunt Mabelle was very close to my father, her brother, who claimed she was his favorite sister. She lived in one-half of a semi-detached house she shared with Uncle Reds on Stanberg Street in Wilson. We left Aunt Doll's house in the country and moved in with Aunt Mabelle. Aunt Mabelle's household consisted of her husband, Uncle Fred, and her three daughters, Alice, Evelyn, and Daisey. I called this Aunt Mabelle's house because she ran things. Uncle Fred loved to nip his alcohol and limped all the more after doing so.

As we came home from school, both sides of the house were filled with the aroma of slices of sweet potato simmering in a skillet. There was also a saucepan of pinto beans bubbling on the stove alongside a pot of string beans. A typical meal from Aunt Mabelle's kitchen also included cornbread and home-churned butter, hot fried flour bread, collard greens with fatback, molasses, and sweet iced tea. Chickens were caught, their necks wrung, plucked, and fried in lard. Now that woman could cook!

The best part of living with Aunt Mabelle was being around her adventurous daughters. They all talked back to the adults, including sass-mouthing our mean stepmother, Betty.

In the summertime, we could walk to the fair from Aunt Mabelle's house. Although we didn't have money to enjoy ourselves as other kids did, it was just wonderful getting away from Betty. At that time, she was always fussing and beating us down like dogs. My aunts would fight for us, but they couldn't provide us with twenty-four-hour protection from the abuse. Betty would beat us that much harder when she was out of their sight. It was as if we got a revenge whipping if anybody dared express care for us. Around the same time, they also became self-appointed guardians over my infant cousin, Jerry.

My brother and I sometimes would spend time around our father's brother, Uncle Oliver, better known to the family as Uncle Coke. We never knew where he got the name Coke. Uncle Coke's wife, my Aunt Magdalena, used to feel sorry about the way my brother and I were treated. She would protect us and feed us. What I remember most are the banana sandwiches Aunt Magdalena used to make for my brother and me. Although they weren't exactly what we liked, she did her best to make sure we were not starved. She also showed us love—which was never shown by Betty or Coley Sr.

Despite all this support from our aunts, we were still subject to brutality at home. When he was nine, my brother Coley Jr. ran away after another brutal beating by our stepmother. He ran from our house through the woods, hiding there for several hours. This was the first time either of us had attempted to get away from our father and stepmother. He returned home just as night was falling, defeated by his own fear of the dark with no place to go.

New clothes arrived just twice a year, right before Christmas and Easter. They were sent by my biological mom in Delaware, who now had a separate family that didn't include us. My mean stepmother would only let me wear the new clothes to church, which meant I would end up growing out of the clothes before getting to really enjoy them.

Somehow my father, Coley Sr., and Betty acquired an abandoned two-story schoolhouse just outside of Wilson. This became home for my brother and me for a while. This was also the largest dwelling we had lived in as a family. We used a section of this schoolhouse to live in. We only occupied two cold rooms on the first floor of this building. A small coal stove was the only source of heat. Around the same time, they also became self-appointed guardians over my infant cousin, Jerry. Jerry came from our biological mom's sister. When it came to Jerry, I never understood why anyone would surrender a child to a woman as mean as my stepmother. Particularly given the history that my mother and Betty shared.

Although I was just a child in third grade, I ended up caring for the infant. His dirty cloth diapers had to be changed, and because it was so cold during the winter, I often had to break them free of ice just to shake the feces from them before they could be washed. Betty made sure that I scrubbed them until they were snow-white, clean enough to pass her scrutiny. If they were acceptable to her, I would hang them on the clothesline in the yard, usually in the dark. Often, in the winter, the wet nappies would freeze before I could secure them to the line with clothespins.

This was how it worked with these people: they would bring other people's children to live in the household they could barely afford. There were no adoption papers. Whoever the oldest child was, which in this case was me, became responsible for taking care of the younger children. In essence, I was a mother before I was out of grade school. This, I felt, robbed me of my childhood. Instead of playing with other children or doing childish things, I focused on adult responsibilities. I was doing everything a woman would despite being a child myself.

It's no wonder my body has so much arthritis and aches so badly to this day. I was doing grown-up work from an early age.

The abandoned school they had forcibly made home was uncomfortable for me. The stove cranked out the heat in an unhealthy way. It barely heated the one room we called home. We would, at times, catch coughing fits or have soot-stained clothes because there was no venting for the coal dust and black exhaust. By the time environmental laws and rules banished indoor stoves without vents, the damage had been done. I would struggle with respiratory ailments for the rest of my life.

Meanwhile my father made sure he presented himself as a contradiction to the way we lived. Whatever job he had, he made sure he was dressed to kill, with spiffy suits and well-shined shoes. Even when he smiled, what was shown was a row of glittery gold-embossed teeth. I can't say I admired him. What kind of man would show himself off while his family suffered and went without basic necessities?

We ate powdered eggs, bland peanut butter and crackers, and anything distributed by the government. I distinctly remember those extremely cold mornings, with wads of paper placed in the bottom of my very second-hand Saddleback shoes, which sloshed in the snow with every step toward the bus stop. Coley Jr. and I used to clutch our peanut butter crackers, tears flowing from our eyes against the brittle wind. I remember one morning, on the long walk to the bus stop, being so fed up with our conditions that I stopped and sat on the road. I refused to walk another step. My brother kept begging me to get up, but I suppose at that point, I thought I might be warmer if I sat down and wrapped my arms around myself. My brother begged me to come on, saying that the bus would leave us. He persuaded me eventually, and I got on the bus en route to Elvey Street Elementary School.

I attended first and second grades in Delaware. All systems were segregated back then, but in North Carolina, neither the books nor the bus rides were free. It's amazing how things were so different and noticeable to me as a child. Any other child would have struggled under the circumstances of my early life. Between the brutal beatings, food insecurity, and poor living conditions, it's a wonder I was not behind in school. Despite all this adversity, I received good grades and continued to do so until I graduated high school. I considered school an outlet for what I was going through every day. My dedication and hard work are what would see me through even the worst of times. Perseverance was a big factor in saving my life from ruin.

I was about five years old when my grandmother, Grandmom Hattie, passed. She was my mother's mother. My brother Coley Jr. and I loved that woman. Life at Grandmom's house was good. We ate delicious hot cooked meals three times every day. In addition to cooking scrumptious meals, she made great homemade desserts like homemade rice pudding, cakes, pies, etc. We had it going on, but after she passed, life changed. It was then that we experienced a dramatic downturn in many respects. Coley Jr. and I moved from Delaware after her passing to North Carolina with Coley Sr. and Betty.

Now in Boston, living with my father's youngest brother, Uncle Ralph, we were lucky if we even got breakfast before having to head off to school. We were still starving, but we did occasionally get to eat delicious Kosher hot dogs Uncle Ralph brought home. He would ration them out amongst the family as if we were standing in a food bank line. While in Boston, I would often think back to times in Delaware when Grandpop brought home old stale bread and put it in a big barrel that was located behind the kitchen door so it wouldn't swing open. The kitchen had a downward-sloping floor so that the door wouldn't open with any gust, letting in the cold. In the morning, we had to hurry downstairs when called to get ready for school. The only heat in the big house we lived in came from a woodstove located downstairs with a hole cut in the ceiling to let heat travel upstairs, where there were two large bedrooms.

Everything was so different up north. The biggest difference was how everyone spoke. I felt like a country bumpkin when I tripped over little words such as "the" or "and." For instance, up north, everyone drank "tonic" instead of "soda." It all required quick adaptation to be successful in school or navigate our new surroundings.

We were not allowed to complain about the cold (and up north, it got much colder than we were used to down south). If we did complain, Grandpop would say, "Well, you need to get a move on." He equated being cold to being lazy. He felt because he provided a roof over our heads and gave us food to eat, he reserved the right to discipline us however he chose.

Grandpop was a spry old man. He could kick his leg over the top of our heads to demonstrate his agility. He was fortunate to be alive, often telling us that he was born prematurely in a time when there weren't incubators. The truth was, he didn't have an exact date he was born, but we guess that it was around the year 1900. Records of birth weren't kept that well during his era, particularly for people of color. He only estimated it by the seasons when his birth might've been. I myself never had a birthday party until I was twenty-one years old.

He was very strong and an extremely hard worker despite his size, and when he said to do something, he meant for us to do it without any hesitation. I remember one particular school morning when Grandpop called upstairs for us. I was so cold and just waking up. It took me longer to get going. Without warning, he came up the stairs to hurry me along. The next thing I knew, he had lifted my little body up with a kick of his big black, thigh-high workman's wader rubber boots. The boots covered all the way over his knees. My body tumbled down the whole flight of stairs. He looked at me without any remorse or pity and repeated his favorite line: "When I say get a move on, I mean get a move on."

My back was badly bruised and took a long time to heal. He didn't care if you were a boy or girl, big or small, young or old. If you didn't move fast enough, he would help you move.

We didn't have running water in the house, which made our morning and evening routines that much longer. There was a hand pump located outside the backdoor of the house. Choking the pump at night, when temperatures had dropped, the water was so chilly that it would drain back down into the well. Just as it was necessary to choke the pump at night, it was a requirement to catch the pump in the morning so the water would start flowing again. It was important to do this so that all the household chores and cooking could be done. Otherwise, we would have to go the day without running water.

If this wasn't done correctly, the water in the galvanized pipe would freeze, and there was a whole different process to get the water flowing again. We didn't allow that to happen too often, as freezing the pipes led to some serious reprimanding by Grandpop. And we didn't want any more bruises or beatings.

To get hot water, we would have to heat a large kettle on top of the wood-burning cook stove. We'd then pour it into a foot tub or sometimes a large basin and mix it with cold water in order to take our baths. There was no money for deodorant or toothpaste, so we used Arm & Hammer baking soda for those purposes. Regardless of how poverty-stricken we were, we neither had bad breath nor stank. That just wasn't permitted.

We used the grease left over from meat to rub on our arms and legs instead of lotion, so there wasn't any husk on us. My mother and aunts used the same lard on their hair for styling. But by the time I came along, haircare products like Dixie Peach, Royal Crown, and Apex were being used. The matriarchs would use these in my hair with a stiff brush. They dyed my fire-engine red hair to a sand brown by using leftover coffee grounds.

Coley Jr. and I walked over three miles to school and did the same when coming home from school. It didn't matter if the temperature was zero degrees or one hundred degrees—we walked. Occasionally, Grandpop would come along on our way to school on a cold morning and tell us to hop in his old raggedy truck. It was just as cold inside the truck as it was outside. The only benefit was we arrived at school a bit faster. As I crawled into the old truck, I would pray Grandpop didn't see the brown paper bag lying alongside the road where I had thrown it. The lunch bag had hard, stale, seeded day-old bread with strawberry preserves (or whichever flavored jam we had in the house). There was no wax paper to wrap the sandwiches in and definitely no tinsel paper, which is now called aluminum foil. We had to remain humble and take what was available or go hungry. Most of the time, the latter was my choice, especially if the jam had those little seeds in it.

During this time, there weren't any food stamps or subsidized lunches. Being able to gather twenty-five cents for a hot lunch at the school was next to impossible. If I did manage to scrap together some change, I looked forward to getting whatever the school provided. My favorites were these tiny little biscuits Ms. Naomi, the school cook, would make. We didn't have a cafeteria, just Ms. Naomi. These little biscuits were only as big as half of a silver dollar, but they were so savory on my young malnourished palate.

When we were living in North Carolina years before with my father's sisters, things weren't much better. My cousins teased me on a recent visit back to town about eating collard green sandwiches or fat back, the grease running down my childhood face. I reminded them that we were so hungry back then that we ate whatever we could.

Life in this house was similar to life down south. There wasn't a lot of money, and I'm not sure if my father contributed to food and/or housing while we lived there. He always wanted to show his gold teeth and stayed dressed up, always riding in nice cars that he couldn't afford. Those were his priorities at all times.

My brother and I almost got arrested for stealing shortly after we got to Boston. We were exploring the city. Its streetlights and sidewalks were very different from those down south. In the dusk of night, we walked about fifteen city blocks on Massachusetts Avenue, unconcerned for our safety. Headed toward Cambridge, we happened upon a First National Grocery Store, which was just on the other side of the busy median. After sprinting down the highway in our oversized winter coats, our hungry feet led us down the aisles in the store. We began to fill our jackets up with food. We came out about ten pounds heavier than we went in. We stole cans of spaghetti and meatballs and Spam. But we were unsure of the route back to the apartment, and the streetlights were already on as night hid our way. So we took the bounty back the way we came to the best of our young memories. Our uncle Ralph and the others were up in arms because no one knew where we had disappeared in this big city. By the time we reached the apartment, our hearts were pounding, and our palms were sweating with worry. We tiptoed inside, careful not to signify to anyone our long journey. Uncle Ralph beat us unmercifully with an extension cord that night. It appeared we were born to be punching bags for the hostile to beat on.

I later learned that Uncle Ralph harbored a lot of anger because he was haunted by his own demons. It was quietly known within the community that he was gay. Having never really expressed his sexuality, he built up a lot of anger. Of course, my father and Betty stood by as he took that anger out on us helpless, starving thieves.

My favorite part of attending school in Boston was being able to take home economics in fourth grade. We sewed ponchos and aprons. We made homemade peanut brittle and fudge. I took advanced classes like French and Chemistry, all of which made me more advanced than students in Delaware or North Carolina. Despite my advanced academic life, we still lived in poverty, having cheap bologna or potted meat for our lunches. To this day, I never add either of these items to my grocery list. Looking back, I can see that I truly was a gifted student to have survived and excelled despite the lack of proper nutrition. Even with the abuse at home, I remained an Honor Roll student, making straight As in all coursework. My self-belief didn't always allow me to see myself as gifted, but I am grateful that now I finally do.

Although living in Boston provided many positive opportunities, my brother and I were abused so badly that we didn't enjoy life. My brother was the first to leave Boston and return to Delaware. He had gotten into serious mischief with his friend Sammy, a real Bostonian with a passion for trouble-making. The two of them began robbing parking meters around town. When Betty found out what Coley Jr. was doing, she would count out the money and keep it in her handkerchief. She'd then turn some of the money in on Sundays at church to look like a good saint. But it wasn't all honest. She would also pay bills and buy food with the other half of the stolen money. Coley Jr.'s misdemeanors grew so bad that I was afraid my brother would be killed by the police or that something tragic was going to happen to him if he found himself on the wrong side of the wrong crowd. When the authorities finally got involved, Betty advocated for him to go to a reformatory school, washing her hands of any guilt or awareness of his crimes.

They put him on a train to downtown Boston to the precinct. But he ran away from the police, leaping from the moving train car in a desperate attempt to flee being locked up. He made his way back to the apartment with head-to-toe scrapes and bruises. He looked to me like he had leprosy. I called my mom in Delaware and begged her to call the authorities in Boston and say that she wanted my brother "sent back to his real mother in Delaware." I made her promise to me that she would swear to them she could handle his misbehavior and straighten him out. I hated to see my brother leave me, but I also wanted him to live. This was something I knew he could not do if he stayed in Boston.

After he left Boston was when I really caught hell as far as the abuse went. I was the only laborer and whipping post in the house. There was no mercy. I was fortunate to still be on two legs four years later when we took a summer vacation to Delaware. This trip eventually became a ritual. After all, Betty and Coley Sr. had to return to their respective hometowns to show off just how prosperous they had become. They would brag about their new car and how much money they were making, all with delusions and stories of how well they were doing in the big city.

As children, we had to perpetuate their lies. Once I had to run down the street to pull the fire alarm because they hadn't paid the electric bill. The candles we burned in order to see after sundown had caught the apartment on fire. Fortunately, the fire trucks showed up in record time and put the fire out. However, the landlord now knew that there was no electricity in the second-floor apartment we resided in, and the authorities now knew underaged children were being left alone at night. Even though I had acted responsibly, the fire department tore out some of the wall plaster, for which I was now to blame. By this time, there was no such thing as a light chastising in this house. Betty tried to literally kill me. She never had children of her own, and according to her sister, she never wanted children. And she made that clear every time I felt her hands on me.

Even our father treated us with contempt. I remember watching this man take a knife and peel a Golden Delicious apple so perfectly, never breaking the spiral, in front of me. I watched with glittering eyes, wanting a slice of that sweet-smelling fruit, only to be given the peels to eat as he sat in front of us, enjoying the entire apple slice by slice. It was the same when a watermelon was cut. I used to wonder how many miniature pieces could be cut from a watermelon, feeling the torture on a summer day, wanting to taste the forbidden fruit. He'd talk it out. First, he was going to eat the "heart" of the watermelon, all the while describing just how sweet and delicious the watermelon was. Then he would proceed to cut the miniature pieces. And I'd better not ask for another piece. Even asking would get us yelled at and possibly beaten senseless.

This upbringing made me very grateful for what I have in life. Despite my impoverished beginnings and even financial burdens later in life, I ended up finding success and becoming a generous person. I take a lot of inspiration from Joseph in the Bible, who, despite being betrayed by his family, eventually became the savior of his family. In times of famine in our lives, we must still remember that God can still do much with little. Even if that little is a bag of peanut butter crackers.

# Survival

*"My God, my God, why have you forsaken me?*
*Why are you so far from helping me*
*and from the words of my groaning?"*

Psalm 22:1 NKJV

Leaving Boston became a reality only after running away from home as a teenager. At this time, all of my siblings from my mother were living with my mom in Delaware, all of whom I saw only once a year during that week-long summer visit. After begging on multiple occasions to be reunited with my family in Delaware, I took desperate measures when it was clear that I would never be granted that opportunity. When I first had the idea to escape this bondage, I was terrified at the thought. Could I really do it? My safe haven, which happened to be directly across the street, was my best girlfriend's house. I hid away there for about a week but was made to return to the inferno that I was determined to escape from at any cost.

I was enduring sexual, mental, and physical abuse every day. I had no one to vent to or help me. I felt like a mouse in a trap and needed a way out. The man who was supposed to be my biological father was responsible for most of the sexual abuse. Every chance he got, whenever he chose, Coley Sr. would make his awful assault on me. Sometimes I would be awakened out of my sleep, and he would take me to his bed and have his way with me. He would whisper to me never to tell anyone and then send me to the bathroom to pee immediately after he finished. I always felt dirty, never clean enough. It is a feeling I still struggle to rid myself of completely. At the time, I believed my life would always be this way. The scars will follow me to my grave.

The church rituals remained the same during these trying years. Despite the repeated disgusting sexual encounters, the brutal daily beatings, and the vulgar name-callings, I had to attend church two to three nights a week. Each service was usually three to four hours long. In addition to the weeknights, there were three services every Sunday, which lasted from nine in the morning to eleven at night. I never understood or saw the benefit of so much church. These Christians demonstrated the opposite of what they professed. I never saw love, peace, or any Christ-like characteristics in them. I did, however, learn the true meaning of long-suffering.

Before leaving for church, as well as returning from church, the profanity began with my stepmother yelling. "Pig Bugger" was one of her favorites (though the other curses were equally as bad). I could not understand how she could draw breath to curse like a sailor and still testify God's holiness out of the same mouth. I would pray to God something like, "If you do exist, God, how can this be? You're supposed to be watching everything, but day after day, you allow this to go on in my life, and nothing changes."

I also wondered how the other people, who were supposed to be Christians, could not see such hypocrisy in their actions too. Oftentimes my bruises and scars were so plain to see that it bothered me that no one around us questioned their source. Our dramatic home life was tattooed across my body, but it seemed no one cared about my condition. The more I pondered the craziness, the worse it appeared to get. And so I remained confused and humiliated, enduring the hurricane of the hurt they caused.

During these teenage years, prior to leaving Boston, I was a big thrift store shopper. This was my one spot of joy and reprieve. After my stepmother and my so-called father left for work at five o'clock each evening, I hailed a taxi for them every day as another part of my unpaid responsibilities. This way I knew for sure that they were gone. I would run errands for the elderly people who lived in my apartment building. I would earn a little cash by getting the daily paper or whatever they needed to get from the convenience store. Each trip to the store would yield twenty-five to fifty cents. Although the convenience store was directly across the street from my apartment, crossing the busy median on Massachusetts Avenue was the most difficult part of it all, particularly at five o'clock at rush hour.

After my evening of errands, I would walk away with enough cash to buy a few pieces of clothing from the thrift store (and sometimes a snack from the corner store). This was my form of appeasement to get through another day of the inferno I was living in at this time. But even running errands to earn a little money to buy clothes to wear was risky. There was a white man who worked in the store who would try to fondle my body every time I stopped in the store. I would time my visits so that as many people would be in the store at the same time so that I could quickly pay for my stuff before my witnesses left.

I would pray every day for God to please help me and take me away from this miserable place. Sometimes I even felt God didn't care. Often I questioned why I was even born. I would think of my sister and brothers with my mother enjoying their life; meanwhile, I was abandoned in this miserable city, enduring hardships.

In addition to all this, I remained Cinderella at home. I had to keep the house spotless to meet my stepmother's requirements. I prepared all the meals unless Betty felt like cooking. I got on my knees and diligently washed her delicate, dirty undergarments in a bathtub to meet her standards. If, by chance, the girdle was not white enough or clean enough when she inspected it, my wicked stepmother would take those wet nylon garments and slap me across the face with them. I would have to wash them again until she was pleased.

Any of the younger children in the house were also my responsibility to care for daily. I wasn't allowed to visit friends after school, go to movies, or attend social events. There was definitely no tolerance for talking to boys. God forbid! Although I was, on occasion, accused of such, I was too afraid to flirt. I didn't have an interest in exploring dating as a teen due to the frequent rapes of my so-called father. I also had no clue how one actually became pregnant. I knew that eventually, I was going to start my menstrual cycle, according to what I was reading and hearing, but I had no one to talk to or guide me into womanhood.

I'm grateful for that final summer, while on my trip to Delaware, that my luck began to change, and I would no longer be forced to live in this house of torture.

As I mentioned at the start of this book, I am the second oldest of my mother's seven children. The seven consisted of five sons and two daughters. One summer in Delaware, I was telling my sister Brenda everything that was happening in Boston and about my runaway attempts. I told her I simply couldn't bear being in the house with Betty and Coley Sr. any longer. She knew everything about what was really going on. I would confide in her, but it didn't matter, sad or not; I was going back to Boston. It was Brenda, who was my mother's favorite, who whispered in our mother's ear to not make me go back. My mother said, "I've fought this woman before, on church grounds even. I'll fight her again!"

I'm so grateful my mother listened to my sister and put her foot down, for after she had some choice words with my father and stepmother, they agreed to let me stay in Delaware permanently. But I could never shake the fear that one day my mother might change her mind and send me back to Boston. Thank God that never happened.

Coley Jr., or Junior as he was mostly called, is only thirteen months older than me. It was always assumed I was the oldest. I suppose this was because I was always the leader between him and me. He has always been somewhat quiet and reserved. I always had that boss-like and take-charge attitude, whereas he, with the exception of some occasions like that cold morning walk to the bus, preferred to be more easygoing. As a child, I don't recall being afraid of anything. Besides our horrific stepparents and abusers, there wasn't much that scared me. Coley Jr., however, would run from a fight with a fly.

Back then, we would walk three miles to school, passing the home of this chubby white boy who would approach us every day with taunts and threats because we were Black. Coley Jr. would see him coming and take off running, yelling behind him at me, "Come on, sis!" But I was determined to stand my ground and prove to this racist kid that I wasn't afraid of him. I would deliberately walk as slowly as I could, daring him to come one step closer.

Coley Jr. would let the fear of failure grip him when it came to school studies, thereby not allowing him to make better grades. I, on the other hand, made good grades with little effort. I would try to tutor my brother, but he would become frustrated, and the material just wouldn't stick. Of my siblings, Coley Jr. and I were the closest. We shared the same biological father, and throughout our childhood, we were together, always in the shuffling from home to home.

Coley Jr. and I suffered so much abuse from Coley Sr. and Betty that we formed an everlasting bond. We both often say it's a wonder that we are still alive. We had to look out for each other and safeguard each other as best as we could when traveling from north to south year in and year out. Before we left Delaware, I remember fighting a girl who supposedly fancied Coley Jr. as a boyfriend. I really don't know how the argument or fight began. To be honest, it was probably my fault. I was the one most likely to have said something or done something to start the incident. Now, I'm not bragging, and I'm not necessarily proud of this, but let's just say she wasn't hanging around after that fight. If I started something, I usually finished it. This is one of the few physical altercations I remember instigating in my life. At that time, I was a hurting little girl living with so much anger, as much was misdirected my way. Fighting her helped vent my rage and release some of the pain and frustration I was holding on to. I did not know at that time the correct way to handle my emotions. I have since learned that hurt people hurt people. And much of my life, I've been trying to prove that this is not always the case.

My brother, however, did continue to hurt people, including himself. He struggled in school and made some poor choices during his young life because he didn't have a place to vent. I think the same is true for a lot of young Black men in America. He never said much or expressed his feelings. Neither of us was ever allowed to voice or express our feelings or our opinions about anything. Whereas I strove for outward success, Coley Jr. internalized what we were going through. I'm not quite sure if my brother had a relationship with God at the time, given our upbringing in the church was tricky at times. As close as we were, I should have confessed to him that I felt guilty for not giving him the space to express what he was going through. We were both in survival mode, truth be told. We didn't have time to spend talking about spiritual or emotional matters.

We both were mandated to spend every Sunday in church. From nine a.m. Sunday morning to ten or eleven p.m. Sunday night, we were there. On occasion, we spent most Saturdays in church as well. There were also a couple of weeknights that sometimes dragged into eleven p.m., the adults blatantly not considering the homework we children had to do. We were expected to be up early and ready for school the next day. My guess is that because of the dysfunctions we were experiencing, my brother probably checked out when it came to spirituality. I won't say he stopped believing in God—only he knows that—but he most likely had a difficult time trying to conceive of a

God who allowed our horrendous circumstances. That was hard for me too. He most likely had the same questions as I did about how God and why God permitted all we were going through as innocent children.

Once we were staying with my grandpop's second wife, who cared for us like her own. We called her Mom Sarah. Though she never had any grandchildren, she loved my brother and me unconditionally. On a particular day, Coley Jr. decided to play with matches and mistakenly set the woods on fire. I remember seeing big billows of smoke and flame burning behind us as we ran inside to tell Mom Sarah. She ended up calling the fire department. Poor Coley Jr. suffered a few whippings from Mom Sarah, who used a huge nurse's shoe. These shoes looked like tanks looming over him. I felt bad for my brother and was torn as to whether I had done the right thing by telling her what he had done to Grandpop's woods. Now, looking back on it, we just burst out in laughter. However, when it was happening, it was not funny to either of us. During the rest of Mom Sarah's life, she never forgot that ordeal, and she would laugh along with us until her dying day anytime we brought it up.

I'm grateful that after my brother's failed attempt to run away from law enforcement by jumping out of a moving train, God spared his life. I made the necessary contacts to get him out of Boston and back to Delaware, where he changed his entire lifestyle and became an asset to society instead of a liability. My brother Coley Jr. quit school and became a father at sixteen. At the time, it seemed strange, but I now fully understand because we both were in search of real love. Real love and care were so scarce for us our whole lives. My brother, after being influenced by an older man named Mr. Fred Hall, stopped doing minimum-pay farming and joined the military to take care of his soon-to-be son. My brother enlisted in ATV17 and did very well in his military career, reaching the rank of First Sergeant before retiring with close to twenty-five years of productive service in the

United States Army. He served in countries as far away as Germany and Iraq. He got married and successfully raised four wonderful sons.

In later years, Coley Jr. dedicated his life to God and took on many roles in the church. He often helps with planning and cooking for special events or giving remarks during service. Although my brother's health has been compromised over the last three years or so, he is full of faith and hasn't given up. Now I see his faith stronger than ever. Whenever I ask him how he's doing, he tells me he's "hanging in there." And that's what we're all trying to do: just "hang in there."

I am so grateful my brother didn't end up like Sammy, his best friend in Boston, who was later shot to death. I'm also grateful Betty and Coley Sr. weren't able to cash in those life insurance policies they had on us.

# Family

*"Although Joseph recognized his brothers,*
*they did not recognize him.*
*Then he remembered his dreams about them..."*

Genesis 42:8–9 NIV

As for my other siblings, they resided with our biological mother, who lived in Delaware. We saw our other siblings for only one week once a year. This was hardly enough time for us to get to know each other or for us to bond. Traveling from Boston to visit our mother was always a circus for Betty and Coley Sr. I jokingly called it the "Boasting and Bragging Session." They would showcase their new cars, Coley Sr. would dress up in his three-piece suits and shiny shoes, and Betty would make sure she bought us new clothes for this trip (regardless of how cheap or ill-fitted they were).

Coley Sr. and Betty attested they didn't want any children, which is why they treated us so poorly to begin with. It was difficult for us, however, to know that our other half-siblings were living free of the abuse and neglect we were experiencing. In public (and even to our other family members), it was made to look like we were a normal, happy family.

Henry was born right under me. He was, and is, skilled and gifted. I didn't grow up as close to Henry, though he and I are twenty months apart in age. Henry laughed a lot and always had a strong bass voice, whether he would shout or whisper. I really felt Henry cared very little, if at all, for school. Henry always preferred using his hands to using his brain.

Henry once found himself in serious trouble when he decided to take Mom's radio apart. He was old enough to know better but young enough to allow his curiosity to override his common sense. Coley Jr. and I were staying with Mom as we did every year for the one week in the summer. Henry took the radio Mom had purchased from the man who collected payments on it weekly. This was the way Mom bought furniture and other things for her house. She would find what she liked at Outten Brothers and make payments on it. It might not have been an expensive radio, but I'm sure Henry paid much more in the butt whipping Mom gave him when she discovered he had taken it apart and couldn't put it back together. I suppose he just wanted to see how those voices got in that box.

In my opinion, this situation was part of Henry's skill beginning to manifest. He continued tinkering down through the years, doing mechanic work for himself as well as the entire family. He did so until his health slowed him down later in life. His real occupation was catching chickens, which was not an easy job at all, in some way requiring more skill than fixing a car. He spent his career in the famous chicken houses of Delaware, where farmers fed, watered, and raised chickens before the birds ended up on plates and in restaurants all over the globe.

Henry hated working with Grandpop more than any job he had in his entire life. Early in the morning, before the sun came up, Grandpop would come to pick Henry up. I would be awakened by Henry's crying and moaning. He would plead, saying he didn't want to go. But that didn't matter. Grandpop would gather up Henry along with all the unemployed young men on that road where he lived and take them to work with him on the water. In my opinion, we need more like my Grandpop today. He showed young men by example how to develop into men with good work ethics. He showed them how to manage money and how to become entrepreneurs who were good citizens in the community. Grandpop would permit these young men to buy food, but the remainder of the money they earned came home to be used to pay bills. So few, if any, role models like Grandpop are around today.

Henry and I have never been close, although we are only a few years different in age. Instead, he and Brenda had a bond like Coley Jr.'s and mine. Henry was argumentative with me about everything, yet I have paid fines for him and made numerous sacrifices for him. As recently as my mother's second stroke, he asked me to leave. He felt I wasn't needed to help care for my mother. Some very unkind things were stated to one another. In the end, I remained a caregiver for our mother. Henry's health has declined over the years. He has had strokes and heart issues. I continue to help him in every way I can because he's my brother, and I love him.

Unfortunately, his only child, his son, like my son, found himself incarcerated. Because I was in charge of the education department in the prisons I worked in, he has asked for my advice or help on occasions. Of course, I gladly helped. When his son became gravely ill and only had days to live, he was taken from prison to the hospital, where he was guarded during his stay. The warden said Henry couldn't visit his son. For our family, "no" was not an acceptable answer. I petitioned God and made a few calls. Not only was he allowed to visit his son, but the visit was extended for longer than expected. A few days after that visit, my nephew passed, but at least he and his father got an opportunity to spend quality time together. The takeaway from this was that no matter the situation, continue to give and show love, let go, and let God.

I've always tried to be the best role model for my sister and brothers, though I'm not sure it has always been accepted as such or even appreciated. My only sister, Brenda, is exactly three years and four months younger than me. She was born on July 5. We didn't appear to have had a close relationship for the same reasons as my other siblings who lived with my mom. Coley Jr. didn't mince words with the younger siblings, even being the introvert of the family, and they all respect that. But for the same token, they would resent me for speaking up. With Brenda and me, it was always perceived as simple jealousy; however, it was just sisterly rivalry.

Brenda and I have always found humor in most of what we discuss. We often reflected on those short one-week summer visits we shared. I always viewed my sister as the prettier one. She had a tomboy demeanor, in part because of her four brothers. I also believed she and my brothers lived a better life, which made me jealous. Brenda had such beautiful hair, never needing anything but styling. Her hair was straight without a relaxer and would hang a curl pattern. She was extremely thin too. The only negative about her was that she was constantly coughing from chronic asthma. Despite this, she could run extremely fast. It was next to impossible to catch her, even when she was laughing and coughing mid-sprint. Brenda had a very nice complexion, warm and bright at the same time, like the skin of a pecan. Like me, she was adorned with deep dimples when she smiled (which was most of the time). She giggled all the time, and rightfully so.

Everything about her life was far better than mine. She got to spend time with her mom every day. She was allowed to go outside and play just about whenever she chose to do so. She didn't have to do house chores or take care of other people's babies. Brenda was not being cursed at or beaten every day. But despite our differences, at first we were very close.

It wasn't until I came to live with my mom that she and I began to have that sisterly rivalry. It wasn't that we didn't love each other. But I was attached and wanted to protect my little sister. She, however, wanted to remain independent and felt she needed to show me she could take care of herself. That's when we began to argue.

I used to sew well and often. On occasion, I would make clothes for Brenda, buying the fabric and patterns, whatever I needed to complete the garments. Brenda would upset me by letting her friends wear what I had made for her, with no regard for my sacrifices. She never seemed to appreciate my efforts to show her how much I cared. The more I tried to show my love for her, the more she rejected it.

My brothers, not knowing any better, viewed our spats as mere jealousy. They appeared as boys to get along quite well and had minimal disagreements that could be resolved in a minute. My poor mother would often say that she would rather have all seven boys than have two girls. I'm not quite sure Mom understood what the arguments stemmed from, but she was upset that my sister and I could not get along.

As we grew older and I got married and moved out of my mother's house, Brenda and I did seem to get along much better. We began to meet and have lunch together, and when I would tell my mom about it, she would respond that she couldn't believe it was a civilized meeting where neither of us ended up with food in our faces.

Amazing as it might seem, we both had our firstborns exactly two years to the date apart. Both of our firstborns were boys. Perhaps God has a plan, even when we do not.

Brenda decided to go shopping with me and said we were going "to walk the baby out of her." We shopped from early in the morning when the stores opened until when the stores were closing. Shortly after we got home from shopping, we went to bed early. But I was awakened at some point when Brenda went into labor. While I was extremely happy and excited for her, I wasn't able to be there for encouragement because I was still too tired. I waited until the next day to hear that she had a healthy and successful delivery.

Motherhood was the beginning of a new life for Brenda. Between my mother and me, we assisted in the upbringing of Alvin, her firstborn son. He was a very easygoing and well-mannered boy who never presented any behavior issues. Alvin was nicknamed Ben because it was said he resembled the man on the back of Uncle Ben's rice box.

Everywhere I went, he went. He would come over to my house, which was a few doors down, and stay with me and my children until it was time to go home again. My mother would drop my nephew off at my house without asking and enjoy herself while I was struggling with my own three little boys at that time. My mother was also aware that I was being very severely abused by my husband. It was a lot to carry, but I welcomed Ben every time he came to stay and never grumbled or complained.

Brenda did marry her second son's father, who was in the Navy and was a native of Tennessee. They had a very speedy wedding. I got a call while at work one day to hear Brenda say they were going to a chapel in Maryland to get married. Though I thought that was very quick, there was nothing I could do or say to change her mind. Eventually, he ended up going back to Tennessee, but Brenda didn't want to move. They parted ways but remained married until, eventually, he decided to remarry.

Brenda ended up having another son but wasn't excited about that baby's father. Her last son's father was no better. This man talked a good show, and that was it. I don't recall him buying the baby a bottle of milk or a single pamper. They eventually parted ways too. He took more than he gave. He took her nice Corvette and moved on without any legal action on Brenda's part. Brenda did confide in me how she suffered some abuse but didn't tell anyone but me. We kept each other's secrets quite well, as sisters do.

Brenda ended up doing well for herself as a tax preparator for clients all across the country. She charged steep fees, and people paid. The same fee she charged strangers is the same rate she charged family, which was difficult for me to understand. I now pay an accountant half of what she charged me several years ago. All of her sons are grown, and she has over twelve grandchildren.

Tyrone has had an interesting life. He was always struggling to find himself. He was born after Brenda. I never had many problems with him while we were growing up until he became heavily involved with substances. He has always been the nervous type. He, later in life, decided to join other relatives in spreading untrue stories. However, I call him on the fictitious tales each time I hear them, only for him to deny them. When I defend myself with the facts, he deflects them (which also doesn't work for me). But again, whenever he needs help with anything, I'm there for him too. I love him, and I just don't have the time or energy to engage in negative situations. My plate is always full, trying to do good and help others.

Tyrone married a nice young lady. Her mother and our mother worked together in a poultry factory for several years. He fathered one daughter by his wife, who already had one son when they married. Together by the one daughter, they had one granddaughter. Because he couldn't give up substances, they controlled him, and she ended up divorcing him. Of course, this took a toll on him, and he continued to use substances throughout his successful military and truck-driving careers. Everyone loves him, but he doesn't love himself enough to get clean and stay clean.

The one brother who died about ten years ago as of this writing was extremely intelligent. I've never met anyone who obtained and retained the superior knowledge my brother Melvin could. Melvin was named after his father. Melvin was very close to Tyrone—as Brenda has been to Henry, and Coley Jr. has been to me. It appeared there were three sets of individuals stuck together among my siblings. Melvin was very heavy, so much so that when he was having heart issues after the passing of his lovely wife, Karen, the hospital had to order a special bed to carry his weight.

When they married, Karen had one daughter. Together they had Melissa and Linear. Melvin and Karen attended church often, although he too struggled with substance abuse. Karen was a homebody, while Melvin would stuff his big body into too-small cars and hit the road almost any day he pleased. They both loved children, particularly their two granddaughters and their grandson. Melvin was a great chef and loved cooking as much as he loved eating. He worked in several of the best restaurants in Sussex County, Delaware, which is located close to the resort and beaches in southern Delaware.

Melvin did see a few unfortunate times with his father. I viewed these situations as cruel and unnecessary, probably because of what I had gone through in Boston. Melvin would sometimes forget or leave his jacket on the school bus or at school. His father, Melvin Sr., better known as Bubs, would beat him unmercifully. Just the thought of it made me want to break down and cry. It always seemed his father had difficulty expressing love to him. He never had anything positive to say to him or about him. Even after Melvin had passed, his dad kept bringing up the wrong things Melvin had done to him. It appeared his dad just couldn't let go of the past and stewed on the negative. I'm not sure forgiveness existed in him.

My brother Anthony is the youngest and the most problematic of all. He has refused to work or take care of himself. He believed he was entitled to everything. When he returned home from the Army without an honorable discharge, he lived directly in the back of my mother's house and paid for nothing since. I guess he couldn't conform in the military either. He ran an extension cord to his deplorable mobile home just so that he could use Mom's electricity. He also used my mother's bathroom if and when he showered.

When I came to live with our mother, I did everything for my baby brother as well. Yet, and still, he had no interest in even being polite to me. I've personally watched him disrespect our mother and her husband to the point that they were afraid even to open their door and step outside. Once my mother moved in with me (and her husband was in the nursing home), he immediately moved into their house, taking charge while I continued to pay the bills every month. He is the youngest of the seven, so maybe there is hope yet for him to change and be more considerate of others. Maturity is a process.

If you look at it through the modern lens today, you might assume we were a normal blended family. But really, most of us were born out of wedlock. A patchwork of different people who were themselves broken or hurting in life. While my siblings and I have all aged, it is clear that God had a plan for each of us to leave our mark on this family. I am grateful that we have withstood all the tragedies and triumphs of our youth, some of us better than others.

# Brilliance

*"We ask ourselves,*
*'Who am I to be brilliant, gorgeous, talented, fabulous?'*
*Actually, who are you not to be? You are a child of God."*

—Marianne Williamson

Of course, returning to Delaware came with opportunities to eat better, as my mother was a great cook and always made sure food was available for every meal. However, there wasn't always a chance for me to make any money running errands as there was in Boston. So, if I wanted to buy snacks like cookies or candy from the store, I had to walk four miles, rain or shine. I began to run errands for an old lady or go pick up corn left in the field. My combined earnings were perhaps twenty-five cents for a five-gallon bucket of corn. It wasn't much, but at least it was something.

I began school that year at the William C. Jason Comprehensive High School, an all-Black high school located in southern Delaware, specifically Georgetown, Delaware, better known as the County Seat. The academics were lagging behind compared to the schools in the Commonwealth of Boston; however, the course selection was good. They offered more creative courses like auto mechanics, foreign languages, home economics, and music. Many prominent people were developed at this high school. After I enrolled, it was quickly established that I was so advanced in my studies that I didn't apply myself or study the entire year. I had already completed many of the requirements the other students were just beginning.

I readily made friends and enjoyed social freedom for the first time. I did, however, go to the principal's office once. I had been hanging around with my dearest girlfriend, Tommaine, better known as "Foodie." I'm not sure how we ended up in trouble, but I am sure that Mr. Dix, the principal, had a reputation for paddling students who ended up in his office. He had a big stature and a quiet mannerism. Somehow we managed to talk our way out of the situation, and I vowed never to find myself in that man's office again.

At the end of that year, it was time to change schools again. According to what I was told, the African-American population voted to expedite the integration process, thereby shutting down William C. Jason Comprehensive High School. This school almost immediately became Delaware Technical Community College, with very few required renovations or adjustments. Of course, there were some upsides to attending integrated schools, particularly the financial aspects and allotted budgets. I wasn't as bothered as others who had not previously attended integrated schools. After all, this was the norm for me in Boston, where I had attended integrated schools.

My best friends at this school were Betty Norwood and Linda Gooch. Betty was an Indigenous American Indian who was dating my brother Coley Jr. We would go to Rosedale Beach to see big acts like Betty Mason and James Brown. We would have a wonderful time, the first time in my life I could feel and act my age. My other best friend was Linda Gooch. The Gooches were well-known in this part of Lewes, Delaware. Linda helped me get an after-school job that took me out of the awful cannery where I was working with my aunt. The Gooches were a family with ties to prominent families of non-color that go back generations. I'm not sure why they were so opposed to each other, Linda and Betty, but for whatever reason, they both remained my best friends—and I never let them talk about each other to me.

Lewes High School was in a different part of the county located on the eastern side of the county near the beaches. I recall having to walk along the roads to meet the school bus while watching and waving to my younger siblings as they rode past, riding their school bus with white kids. The students and the faculty at Lewes were not pleased to be entwined with students of color. Some handled it better than others. I believe I also fared well because of my Bostonian accent and fair complexion. As quiet as it was kept, my complexion and other attributes were attributed to my mother's family being from one of the lost Indian tribes of Delaware. Some people knew them as the Moors; however, the correct name of the tribe is the Mitsawokett tribe. However, because my father was African American or Black, I have been classified as African American or Black.

It was also helpful that I joined clubs like the Future Homemakers of America and the Thespians Drama/Acting Club. I was soon placed on the school's secretarial track because of my academic excellence. Before graduation, I worked in the school office and spent one year in the government-run Cedar Program. This was enlightening and advantageous in beginning a career. Not only did it look good on my resume, but the experience of real office work and responsibilities taught me so much about office etiquette and how to dress and navigate workplace politics. I was actually sorry to see such a fun summer come to an end. However, I was looking forward to returning to school with a nice new wardrobe I had purchased with my earnings.

It was then that I expressed interest in attending college after graduation. The guidance counselor I was assigned to was very nice; however, he didn't engage in conversations with me relating to college. To him, a young woman with my aptitude should focus on my strong homemaking skills. In general, there weren't that many students of color placed on the college-bound track. But to say I would be "best suited as a homemaker" was to seal my fate in a home-bound casket. Even though I dreamed of doing more with my life and getting a higher education, I was still young and impressionable. I saw myself based on how others saw me. It reminded me of that scene in the movie *Field of Dreams* when the coach tells the ballplayer that he'd be better off if he focused on a wife. But my mind was too advanced for that. Even if they tried to decide my fate, I had plans to prove them wrong.

Maybe he said that because that day in his office, I was visibly pregnant. It was a common thing then for girls my age to get pregnant around their junior or senior years. Some of my classmates were already married, hitching themselves to boys who were barely ready for fatherhood themselves.

I remember the moment I got pregnant, and while I was seventeen, I wanted to have this baby. I wanted to have the unconditional love that I had never received. I was also in love with John Wright. John was my brother's best friend, a football player on our school team, and good enough to me that I was willing to carry his child.

The most exciting thing of all to me as a teenager was taking driver's education. I wanted the freedom that my driver's license could bring me. A very close friend named Norman was kind enough to teach me how to drive. If I told Norman I wanted a cheese steak sub at midnight, he would find one even if it meant he had to drive fifty miles to another town. I was too young to appreciate a kind guy like Norman.

Looking back, I can see that he thought so much of me. He was about five years older than I was, and I realized later he had offered driving lessons in hopes of becoming more than a friend. Sometimes, when I think of Norman's sweetness, I could kick myself for listening to John when he told me to break things off with Norman. I would not have gone through so much abuse in my marriage if I had chosen him instead. Norman tried to give me the world. By the time I was mature enough to realize this, I had burned that bridge and had hurt him too much. We tried to talk things through one Christmas years later, but it was too late, and he had moved on.

When it was time to take my driving test, my mom arranged for me to take my exam in her man friend's car. I really did not care for this individual who was wealthy, married, and still attracted to other women, though he also had a wife. He had also offered me the opportunity to work in a restaurant he owned, which my mother thought was a nice gesture. But the thing my mother didn't know was that when she wasn't looking, he had the nerve to pinch my breast. He felt that because he had a bit of wealth, he could do whatever he wanted to with whomever he wanted to. I would rather beg for bread than be involved with him. I was so upset to be using his car that I actually failed the driving test. I left a long scratch on the side where I had scraped another car during the exam. Eventually, I tried the test again (with someone else's car) and passed.

Getting a driver's license was major. But for many of my peers, the next milestone was getting engaged. In the heightened period of the Vietnam conflict, many young men were required to register with selective service. Soon afterward, they were sent to training and then off to the battlefield. Most young men were trained for infantry and became foot soldiers, thereby being placed on the front line. This meant a higher likelihood of returning home in a black bag with a tag on their toe. Some returned with missing limbs, dysfunctional minds, and poor attitudes. Worse, some returned hooked on drugs. The only way out of going to battle was acquiring a deferment; this required you were the only son and you were needed to support your family, or you had a medical issue.

Despite the grim realities of Vietnam, so many young people thought they were ready to start families. We, John and I, were in love and too young to understand the marriage vows we were rushing to make. I became pregnant in August of that year and got married in November. I was seventeen.

Two weeks after my eighteenth birthday, I went into labor at my mother-in-law's house. She was actually my husband's grandmother, better known to many as Ma Dear. She was a wonderful woman. She took guardianship of my husband John and his sister Judice when they were kids after their mother passed. His grandmother affectionately fought to have him named Tommy instead of John after his father. I chose to name my son John, completely unaware of what came with his name. Looking back on my unfortunate marriage, perhaps Ma Dear knew something I did not. She knew better than to entertain the thought of having a grandson named John after her son-in-law, but consequently, her great-grandson was named John after his father, my husband, who was the next abuser. Fortunately, my son John knew better and was taught better than to ever abuse anyone, let alone some mother's daughter.

# "Advice from a Tree"

## Author Unknown

Stand tall and be proud.
Go out on a limb.
Reach for the sky.
Adapt to change.
Branch out.
Stay grounded.
Remember your roots.
Drink plenty of water.
Get rid of dead wood.
Be confident.
Never stop growing.
Bend before you break.
Turn over a new leaf.
Enjoy the view.

# Resilience

*"You may shoot me with your words,*
*You may cut me with your eyes,*
*You may kill me with your hatefulness,*
*But still, like air, I'll rise."*

—Maya Angelou

I left home shortly after my eighteenth birthday, newly married with my little baby boy in tow. I began renting a two-bedroom mobile home near the Dover Air Force base. I spent time commuting from central Delaware to southern Delaware because, despite the life choices I decided to make, I was determined to still graduate with my high school class. At age nineteen, after graduating successfully from school, I needed to enter the workforce quickly to make a living. An opening was available for a secretary in the quality control department at General Foods. I applied and got the position. It was my first real job.

At the time, I can see why I thought this would have made life better—to grow up quickly and leave childhood chaos behind me. I could barely wait to turn twenty-one. That was, to me, the magic age where I could do whatever I wanted, go wherever I wanted, and finally be who I wanted. But the budget was tight every week. I didn't receive any government assistance or additional help. My husband,

John, was as young and inexperienced as I was. Instead of buckling down on our finances or working harder as I did, he let himself run wild. He began having affairs outside the marriage soon after we said, "I do." He was also using substances and became abusive toward me.

I overlooked early on in the relationship how different the two of us really were. As has been said, love blinds us to all faults. I can attest to that being the truth. After a while, it was like I had married a total stranger. He was not interested in being a good husband or father. On the other hand, I felt it imperative to keep my family together because of all I had been through. It is for this reason that I ignored all red flags and kept striving to create the family I never had.

But holding all of this inside was hard on me as a young wife, mother, and employee in the corporate world. Things went from bad to really bad. Corporate office life was a lot to contend with. It wasn't at all about how intelligent I was but more about playing the role I was hired for. I was having a hard time navigating office politics and was stressed by the workload. For years, I was showing up to work in turtleneck sweaters to hide bruises. I had to put a smile on my face and walk into the office as if I came from a happy home after being physically abused before leaving home. John would sometimes follow me around and suddenly unleash his big fists down on me, hitting me in the face and breaking my glasses. Then he'd walk off like he had done nothing wrong.

Additionally, I had been troubled with respiratory ailments. I was once knocked out on the gym floor in high school while playing flag football. (Ironically, the blow was dealt by the skinniest girl in class.) Judging by my injuries, I fell back so hard that the doctor thought I had been in an automobile accident. My sinuses and allergies were so messed up that I had to start taking allergy shots every other day. Even though this was years after that incident, these shots started messing with my nervous system, and when I told the company nurse, she called me crazy.

So I had to go from one end of Delaware to the other to find a doctor who could determine the real reason for my health issues. My insurance company said I had to test 80 percent or greater, or I would have to pay the fee for the results. I tested almost 90 percent on all the tests I was given. The only way I could live without allergic reactions to something would be to live in a bubble—and that was highly unlikely.

But maybe my nervous system was alerting me to something more than just allergies. So I had all these things going on and a three-year-old son who was also sick. He had been battling bronchitis and pneumonia for several weeks. The stress of that, on top of my other worries, was compounding by the day. I never saw any of it coming. I came home from the office one day after picking up my son from daycare, and my whole world seemed to have caved in on me. I started to experience what I now know as an anxiety attack. The ambulance was called. I was taken to the hospital emergency room and examined. I was then prescribed Valium and sent home to rest.

I couldn't eat or sleep. I lost so much weight that I could not think clearly from one moment to the next. I was a mess. I stayed at my mom's house for about three weeks to recover, unable to return home to a loveless marriage and the responsibilities of mothering. At that time, my mom shared she had been through a similar period in her life. It was a relief to hear that she too was overwhelmed by the responsibilities of living. After about a week there, I started coming back to myself. I would be watching my son, who was my inspiration and shining light at the end of a dark tunnel. I wanted to get better so that I could care for my son. I really needed to.

My unsympathetic husband would talk behind my back. He would take my paychecks and make jokes about having me committed. To prove them all wrong, I committed to pulling myself together. Even in all my struggles, I would never be on welfare. When the company I was working for sent me to have a mental health evaluation, I sat there on the plush couch, talking to the psychiatrist for at least an hour. He concluded the evaluation by telling me that there was only one thing wrong with me: I would rather hold everything inside and hurt myself than tell people to go to hell. That was his life-changing medical finding.

# Long-Suffering

*The following accounts of domestic violence may be triggering for some, and so I want to encourage those who need to skip this section to do so. My hope is that you will find the same healing that I have despite the hurts that others have caused and the scars that remain for a lifetime.*

---

I went through so much abuse during my childhood that I feel I could write many books to tell the tale. But I fear that would not make for a very comfortable book. The cycle started around age five and continued well into my teens, early twenties, and through my thirties and a portion of my forties. After finally breaking free of the cycle in my forties, the question remains: how did I keep my sanity despite all of it?

I believe that, first and foremost, it was the grace and protection of God, though I wondered many times if even He had abandoned me to the craziness. There were moments in my youthful life when I wondered why I was born. I doubted if anyone loved me or cared anything about me. I wondered if I had a purpose in life and, if I did have a purpose, what that purpose entailed.

One of the reasons I was born was to be a mother. Reflecting, I am glad I decided to become a mother at such an early age. Otherwise

I might have listened to the suicidal voices telling me I should jump out of cars or off bridges. Yes, it was so bad that I did not believe that I could continue living.

Many warning signs were placed directly in my face; however, it has been stated and proven true love overlooks all wrongs. When we feel we are in love or are loved by someone, we look at things with rose-colored glasses. This was the case with me. I had conditioned myself to accept verbal abuse and, to some degree, physical abuse as being the norm. So, when I got hitched with a man in the Army, it made sense that my whole life became as bad as a war. At any point, a bomb could go off.

Early in our marriage, I witnessed John yell at and use profanity with his grandmother. She raised him when his parents died young, and at the time we became newlyweds, she allowed us to live with her. His grandmother had unintentionally let the heating stove run out of oil. Thereby the house became cold. This sweet elderly lady gave everything and made many sacrifices for us. She worked in the summer cleaning the Henlopen Motel in Rehoboth Beach—a job that didn't pay minimum wage. She didn't deserve this disrespect. He went so far as to hit his sister, who pressed charges against him for hitting her during the argument.

I remember getting involved after the argument, ever the dutiful wife, to protect him from the impending mark on his otherwise clean record. I went so far as to research the process of the Board of Pardons in the state, putting together packets and getting him placed on the board's busy calendar to appeal the charges. After all this, I still wasn't sure he'd actually show up. As we walked into the room where the oval table with the nine board members sat in each chair, none of them looked like us. They were anticipating an attorney appearing when John stated he had no attorney. Their next question was who did all this work and prepared all these necessary documents. John pointed to me and said, "My wife."

The group of men looked at me in amazement. They told John I had saved him approximately ten thousand dollars and expressed how impressed they were with my work. The entire process lasted about an hour for them to conclude that they would make their decision by mail within a few weeks. As they had promised, a week later, the favorable decision came, and John was granted his pardon for offensive touching against his sister Judy.

I was always taking care of other people's problems. Cleaning up after his messes was second nature. Another warning sign came on the week of my cousin's wedding. Because I was an excellent seamstress and also made my own clothes, my cousin asked me to make the wedding gown. Bunny, the wife-to-be, and I went shopping for the materials and decided on a nice pattern. I came home, and I began making the gown. When I completed sewing and was taking the gown to have it professionally pressed, John got angry about nothing and proceeded to drag me and the gown across the yard. This was the abuse I endured from my husband. He just decided he wanted to lash out at me anytime, anywhere. That too should have been enough to tell me to leave and never look back, but I was determined to keep my children with their biological father since I never had that opportunity. I had been taught that divorce was like cursing God. So I stayed.

I did manage to complete the gown but never got to the wedding.

The thing about abusive relationships is that they are usually not the first point of abuse for most couples. I tolerated it in part because I was willing to suffer. I had been brainwashed from an early age that it was a carnal sin to divorce, and secondly, the abuse I endured from my paternal figures made me a case study for a marriage that would end up the same. I never witnessed a mom and dad that were together in a healthy relationship, except Mom Hattie and Grandpop. So, it was crucial to me that I did all I could to keep my children with their father, even if that meant sacrificing my happiness and well-being. But John only lived for himself.

Even after that first incident, the abuse did not stop. When Ma Dear died, John and I moved to Dover, Delaware, to be closer to his job, a job that I encouraged him to apply for and believed he could do. I even filled out the application for him. He was hired at General Foods and began this lucrative and gainful employment, where he remained until he retired. At the time, he was struggling more heavily with substance abuse. This was partially due to him becoming acquainted with Arthur Freeman, the union steward who helped him in many situations. His other friend, Arnold Hatton, better known as Hatman, also enabled his drug use. During this time, I considered John a functional addict. He could do drugs and work, but he was becoming unbearable to live with.

First, I never wanted to be home when my husband was home, so I threw myself into work. There was always too much drama with the females calling our home. He would, of course, deny knowing them when, in fact, we both knew that wasn't the case. Around the time I was laid off from my management job, I learned that John had decided to step outside our marriage with someone who worked in the production area where he worked. Eventually, it became clear to me that he was having many affairs.

The second reason it was necessary for me to work every day was that I had to pay bills and take care of my sons. There was no depending on him. He would have an excuse every payday for where the money went.

He would say, "It was because of the taxes that had been taken out," which meant he couldn't bring home much. He would stay out late at night and claim to be working overtime. He would put a few hundred dollars on top of the television for the show so that it would appear to the boys that he was such a big contributor to the household. He'd also lie and say that it was me who took all his money. The children never saw the other side of the story when I asked for and was denied money reserved to take care of the family. Before I had the opportunity to pay any bills, he would go into my purse and take money—and to confront him was to ask for major drama.

He was also extremely jealous and would go into a rage if he saw a man look at me. God forbid if I were to say hello. That would result in a slap, punches, or curses. Sometimes he'd hit me so hard it would knock me down. When my office had Christmas parties and other activities, I would have to sneak and attend behind his back. At the time, I told no one how obsessed and controlling my mate was. While I was often not allowed to leave home without his permission, he, on the other hand, stayed away from home more than he spent time there. The truth of the matter was that it didn't bother me. At least there was peace because he wasn't in the house.

He would come home drunk and stoned in the wee hours of the morning, put hot dogs in a pot of water on the stove, or attempt to reheat the dinner that I had left for him. He would then fall asleep while the food was heating and nearly burn the house down. So many times, by the grace of God, I would wake up and have to open windows and doors throughout an entire house to clear out the smoke while he lay asleep.

It never bothered him to display this behavior in front of our sons. I would explain privately to the boys that this was inappropriate behavior and that they were never to act that way. They knew they would have to answer to me if they ever abused someone, but I continually prayed they were not influenced by our dysfunction.

Now, at nineteen years old, I was working in management for a Fortune 500 company, General Foods, and had a little money with which I wanted to beautify our house. It was clear to me that I needed to make the best of where we were living. On one occasion, I remember asking John to help put curtains up. Because I was so short and he was about six feet two inches tall, it seemed like common sense to ask for help. But this made him angry, sending him into his rage, cursing and fighting me for trying to do something nice to our home.

I would come home from church on Sundays after having a wonderful service, only to prepare Sunday dinner for a husband who would throw it on the floor while he watched football games. On one occasion, he threw a hot plate of food in my face, saying I should never go back to church. His profanity-laced tirade ended in him asking me to fix him another dinner. I felt so humiliated and hurt as my sons looked on; my skin burned with the meal I had just prepared, and my appetite was gone. To this day, I still don't like the Dallas Cowboys, who were John's favorite team. We couldn't move around in the house when they were playing on the television.

For over two decades, this abuse continued. My self-esteem was completely gone. If it hadn't been for my best friend Esther, I probably would not have been able to keep it together as well as I did. She constantly encouraged me and kept my spirits up while I went through this saga in life. Even in all this, I had confided early on in our relationship with my husband about my terrible childhood. It was that much more hurtful when he abused me too. He would go so far as to tell me I was crazy because of my childhood. There was no sympathy or care from him even then, only negative comments regarding a past I was not responsible for. Again, I should have walked out the door much sooner than I did, but I stayed, hoping and believing it would get better one day.

My children were the reason I stayed with this abusive man, and my children were the reason I divorced him. Through the years, I was diligently striving to improve my standard of living but getting nowhere fast. But my sons began to resent their father. He sometimes took them to places where he purchased drugs before they were even teenagers. At that time, they understood what was going on and had enough sense to know something wasn't right. One day, my son told me in secret that his father had purchased some hashish. While I wasn't completely familiar with the drug language, I researched the name and learned that it was a drug stronger than marijuana. No child should have to witness a parent purchasing drugs. This was very disrespectful to me, and the whole thing was simply pitiful: he could not take care of his own children without getting high. This man was abusing substances, which meant he wasn't thinking rationally enough to be a father or husband.

My sons were the ones telling me I needed to get out of the marriage. Although I was spending so much time crying out to God about my marriage, it didn't seem like prayers were being answered until one day when I was watching some TV talk show. In the episode was a woman who killed her abusive husband when she feared for her life. She said something that to this day shakes me to my core: "I can stay here and be killed, or I can do whatever it takes to kill him." That's when I heard this still, small voice in my spirit: "You need to start to prepare to get out of this. You don't want to go to prison." So, I fielded the questions of where to go, how to go, and when to go.

It was supposed to be until death do us part in the case of my marriage. But I didn't want to end up departing this world at my husband's hands. Little did he know I died long ago in that relationship. I knew this time would be different. The next time would be the last time.

On the day my children and I left, John had come into the house in a rage. He had seen a male friend named Gary sitting in our living room, waiting for him to come home. Also sitting there was my grandfather, whom I had served dinner. He peeped in the windows first, as if it wasn't even his house. Finally, when he came in, he cursed, yelled, and choked me. He tossed me around every corner of the house before pulling out his loaded gun and placing it at the temple of my head.

"I will blow the brains out of your head," he said.

My children were looking at the altercation in fear. Finally, my three boys saw my eyes and knew it was time for them to run to the car. When John turned his head to catch his breath in the struggle, my purse was close enough for me to grab. I ran out the door, not even looking back. He could have come to the door and shot me in the back. But at that moment, I didn't care; I was only concerned about my children and getting to freedom.

As my children and I were driving down the road, we were stopped by the police. I had a light out on my car. I was crying as I talked to the officer, explaining what had just happened. He asked where we were headed. I told him I wasn't sure, as this wasn't planned, but I said we would most likely be going to stay at a motel. He gave me a warning for speeding and sent me on my way. My sons and I spent the night in a motel in Dover, Delaware, only forty-five minutes away from our home. We had no time to gather toiletries or clothing, but we made the best of this bad situation. It appeared no one was going to help us. All we had were each other and God.

I had to find some place to go. I ended up staying with one of my brothers, Tyrone. I explained what had happened. He and his wife were in disbelief. Tyrone and I have had our differences, but he was there for me in the most crucial moment of my life. I spent two months sleeping at his and his first wife's house while figuring out what to do with my abusive husband. I wasn't interested in spending time in a shelter with my sons, nor was I going back to the abuse. Although I have been, and will always remain, grateful to him for this safety net he provided during that crucial time, Tyrone and I had some arguments after the summer I lived with him. He became disrespectful while under the influence multiple times, not just to me but to my sons.

My children drifted apart, as it was summer, and they asked to go stay with friends. I conceded but was not comfortable, though I knew I had to figure out something different before the school year started.

I began praying, asking God for refuge and shelter for me and my children. For the first time throughout this long history of abuse, I had to open up and expose what my sons and I had been going through in order to get help. I ended up purchasing a mobile home through my credit union and placed it on my grandparents' property while I obtained a loan to remodel their house. This house was in such deplorable conditions you could literally stand outside the house and push your hand to the inside. There was no inside plumbing or efficient heat, let alone any air conditioning. The house had to undergo major construction just to have the bare necessities. My faith was activated, and it was certainly substantially greater than my budget. I needed a loan to renovate the home quickly. In the same county, however, there was another Barbara Jean Wright. Her credit was in need of repair, and she and her husband had more credit loaned than they could afford. Even with the identity mix-up threatening to deny my loan, God continued to make a way.

My aunt Lydia taught me so much through the decades of abuse and violence. She was closer to me than my mother was. In the months after I left my marriage, Aunt Lydia fed my kids and did what she could to keep me sane in the midst of heartbreak. My aunt Lydia would clean houses and offer me a job to make ends meet during my transition. One of her clients was Mr. Diver, who owned an automobile franchise. He referred me to Mr. Tim Albanese of the Wilmington Savings Fund Society. He's the reason I got a loan, along with Miss Bernice Edwards, who provided an opportunity for me to qualify for what was known as the Decrack loan because of where the house was located.

I had also been granted protection from my husband. Corporal Zopele was personally assigned to me from the Delaware state police force. I remember carrying a card in my purse with the emergency contact information for the domestic violence organization. Fortunately, I never wore my hurt from all the abuse outwardly, and my sons apparently picked up this same trait.

One thing I never did was pretend to my sons that nothing was happening. Rather, I would take these abusive situations as opportunities to teach the boys what not to do in life.

I talked to them about drugs and violence, using their own father's behaviors as firsthand examples of what subsequently happens. I further showed them the thoughtlessness and selfishness that he exhibited by not caring about feeding his family or being irresponsible about paying bills. I hid nothing from them. I suppose I was offering pre-pre-marital counseling before such a thing existed. I taught them to treat young ladies with dignity and respect. I also taught them to enjoy life and not marry anyone's daughter until they were ready. Also, I taught them to not ever neglect their children because they knew firsthand what that felt like.

I have been told that hurt people hurt people. I believe this to be true in most of the situations of my life. I am fortunate that despite all that I have endured, my faith, as well as grace and mercy, have kept me from becoming a stereotype. I was definitely not the stereotypical woman. I only had one regret: I wished I had realized sooner that I was only inviting more abuse and pain into my family situation by remaining married to a man who abused me and didn't care about feeding his family, as well as being irresponsible about paying bills. I also thought about how many innocent women were often killed when they decided to leave this type of man. The best thing that happened from this marriage was my three handsome and intelligent sons. It took much prayer and faith to continue with this marriage and even more faith to decide to end it. I felt like throwing in the towel so many times but was kept bound by the idea that divorce was a sin. But in the same Bible, it also says that God's will for mankind is life and life more abundantly. And I'm so proud to say that I am living in abundance at last.

# *Success*

> *"Success is to be measured not so much by the position that one has reached in life as by the obstacles which he has overcome."*

—Michelle Obama

I've been privileged to be a part of many organizations in my career, and that is something that makes me very grateful. It was through work that I was able to escape the horrors of what was happening at home in my marriage. To understand what else contributed to my success, I reflect back to when I was a high school student. I would often find myself as one of the few people of color in a class or group. This, in the long run, would be beneficial as I entered various positions later in life. Most other students were too fearful or simply not as interested. But I was curious about everything. I wanted to know how the organizations ran and invested time and energy in bridging the gap for others to join as well. Included in these organizations were the Future Homemakers of America as well as Thespians Drama/Acting Club. Most of the time, I would deliberately pick unusual and non-traditional activities that other Black students did not pursue. Breaking down barriers has always been a part of my mission.

I learned to be versatile throughout my education, often having to change between integration and segregation. However different and/or challenging my situation was, I kept my strong desire and willingness to learn. It was that, along with faith in myself, that helped me not only get by but to succeed. It was important to succeed so that I could one day be in a position to help others less fortunate than I was. (Believe it or not, there were others less fortunate than me and my siblings.)

I didn't let the lack of knowledge or experience keep me from being an active participant. No matter what role or job I had, there was always something intriguing to me about the company I worked for and what really happened in the company to bring about various results. I was able to see within the organization's politics and understand rules and by-laws, as well as their origins. Most of what I learned came from reading, which helped me keep my sanity and offered me a way to escape from the abuse.

In my late teens, I remember taking a test before entering the workforce of a Fortune 500 company, General Foods. The test covered learning corporate etiquette conforming to corporate dress codes as well as mannerisms for coworker interaction. Additionally, a skills test was required, which I passed with flying colors. This was my formal training for that fiercely competitive and professional lifestyle. Having a father who never completed grade school, as well as a teenage mother who dropped out of high school, I knew the odds were against my success from the start. With limited funds, I had to make clothes to wear to the office. This was a skill left over from my childhood, and I felt confident in my skills to create outfits that were good enough and fast enough to serve that purpose. In fact, I was so skilled at making my own clothes that everyone assumed I bought them from a store. The women in the office often complimented my clothes. Sometimes, to make a little extra money, I would sew for other colleagues and then use the money to purchase more material for myself.

The job at General Foods provided me with a head start in leadership. My responsibilities were to decide which products were needed in the distribution centers. I looked at how many lines and shifts were needed to supply the distribution centers, then ordered the raw materials and packaging materials for those products. I handled the scheduling of the production workers and lines accordingly while keeping the warehouse space in mind. Now, as I look back on my responsibilities, I see they were pretty heavy. At that time, there weren't too many women in these positions, especially minority women. I was deliberately breaking barriers. I had to fight to get that position and fight to keep it.

Equal opportunity doesn't always lessen the need to fight in corporate America as you strive to advance in most career paths. This was the case for my educational reimbursement as I opted to further my education, which should have been viewed as a positive benefit to the corporation. I met all of the criteria as laid out in the employee manual, but I had to argue to receive this benefit. It was fine when I was working toward an Associate's Degree in Executive Secretarial Science. However, the problem arose when I expressed a desire to continue my education to acquire a Bachelor of Science in Business Administration and a master's in the same so that I could qualify for a promotion to a management position from the secretarial position. I didn't give up, no matter how hard it was to break the barrier.

I needed an explanation as to why the education reimbursement policy was written in the employee handbook, but it excluded me. The personnel director and I had many meetings, and as I often state, the ends justify the means. Needless to say, I received my bachelor's degree and my Master's in Business Administration while employed at General Foods.

Alongside my professional career, I also worked with the NAACP and the Boy Scouts Council. There I could educate others in areas that were important to the betterment of mankind and assist them in improving their standards of living. This role came about when I started attending the Milford Slaughter Neck Branch of the NAACP during one of the busiest times of my life. Mr. Jessie Bevins, who worked at General Foods in the production area at the time I worked in management there, asked me about joining the NAACP. I agreed to attend the NAACP meeting, and it was quickly clear to me why he offered to bring me into the mix. I was soon elected to be the secretary of this branch. At this particular time, I was a true introvert. I was introverted partly because of personal ignorance but also because the brutality of my childhood left me scarred with silence. I stayed with the organization for a number of years, but my membership activity dwindled after the death of Mr. Bevins and several other key branch leaders who passed away.

While volunteering as secretary for the NAACP, I was also elected president of the Jello Federal Credit Union. Now, I knew nothing about credit unions, but that was not a deterrent from my jumping in with two eager hands. I became one of the top officials of this million-dollar credit union. I worked side by side with the credit union manager, eventually replacing her in that role. Having to terminate my credit union manager tore at my heart. Though I learned a lot from her, the credit union was stagnant under her leadership and needed to offer the members more opportunities for growth.

I occupied and retained the credit union presidential seat for five consecutive years, at which time I was responsible for chairing meetings, evaluating staff, and other responsibilities. During this period, membership grew, thus increasing assets. I was able to help the community become more knowledgeable about credit unions as well as their finances in general. Additionally, we went from a small operation being run out of a General Foods building to purchasing a three-million-dollar office building off-site.

Shortly after this milestone, I began divorce proceedings.

While experiencing the greatest career success of my life, I suddenly felt myself in a world of another personal storm. I had always signed for my ex-husband to withdraw funds from his Thrift Investment account. However, on one occasion, he refused to sign for me to withdraw funds from my Thrift Investment account for our boys, who were just starting to drive. During this era, one partner needed to let the other spouse know when funds were being withdrawn. At the time, the economy was so bad that gas was overpriced and being rationed. This was also the time that when the oil man came to deliver, you had to pay the charge on the spot. I had already taken out a renovation loan on my home for my children and me to live in, and on this occasion, I was running low and needed the funds for this purpose. Now, because my ex-husband refused to sign for me, I signed his name without him knowing. When he found out, he had me arrested for forgery. I had to go to the City of Dover to turn myself in. I was given a mug shot and fingerprinted like a criminal. I was handcuffed to a bench at the station with a puddle of tears in my lap from the humiliation.

When I was released from the police station, I told my aunt Lydia that I was finished with this man for good. There was no love left between us. As many times as he had stolen money from me and as many checks as he had signed my name to, I was outraged that he would have the nerve to stoop to this level. This arrest could have been excessively damaging to my reputation (which is one reason my soon-to-be ex-husband called the police). Thanks to my good standing in the community, help from family, and my organizational involvement, I was able to easily acquire the funds needed to take care of the boys. But I was already one foot out of the door, having filed for divorce. He was hurt because he could no longer hurt me or use me.

Years prior to the divorce being finalized, I had returned home from a business trip in New Jersey when my sons told me my aunt

Lydia wanted me to call her as soon as I walked in the door. Aunt Lydia was the same woman who had helped me leave that marriage and find cleaning jobs when I was strapped for cash. When I called her back, she was working at that moment but asked me to meet her at her house in an hour.

I arrived at Aunt Lydia's house an hour later, as she had asked. She pulled out a newspaper containing an article that showed John's arrest for possession of cocaine. She explained that she had saved the article for me to read myself because she knew I was the type of person who had to see it in black and white ink. Seeing this allowed me to rebuild my life in a meaningful way. It was ironic that I was also featured in the exact same newspaper on the exact same day as a campaigning candidate for the school board.

In addition to volunteering my services to the NAACP and serving as president of the Jello Federal Credit Union, I was approached about serving as a board member in our local school district, the Cape Henlopen School District. This happened to be the same school district I graduated from several years prior and where my children at present were attending. I had never given this position any thought, and although I didn't really have an idea of what would be required of me as a board member, I decided to pursue yet another opportunity to help someone, though I knew nothing about politics.

I was campaigning around the neighborhood, which required that I attend many meetings and do presentations. I would walk what seemed like a never-ending path to talk to people face-to-face and ask for votes. Classmates who attended high school with me were working as hard as I was in my campaign. I had so much help from friends, and I didn't even know I had such a strong network. Most of the people who supported me were basing some of it on the way I spoke with power and articulation. I won by a landslide, beating out Mr. Levy, who was very popular in the community and a successful sports apparel print shop owner.

After being released from General Foods, I had some severance pay to carry me until I entered the education world. Companies at the time were downsizing, and a lot of the niceties we experienced as employees were cut in the mergers. I would sit at my desk, and I would see the person in front of me go into the manager's office and come out with tears in their eyes. The same thing happened to the one in back of me, then the ones to either side of me. Then, one day, they asked me to train a person I knew would soon be my replacement.

I can look back at this time in my life and truly say that God always has a plan. My supervisor asked to speak with me on the day I had surgery. I knew what was coming. They sent a white stretch limousine to take me to the workplace, which was General Foods. The supervisor came out to open the door for me. Inside the office, there was a table of managers seated. They asked if I knew why I was there.

"Yes, I do, because you're going to terminate me today," I said, knowing I would be in education soon and confident as a queen.

They asked if I had any questions for them, and I said, "Yes. How much is my severance pay, and when does it start?"

It was thirty-five thousand dollars, more than enough to cover me until I started teaching. The month they terminated me was the same month I was offered substitute training in a school district. It was the same high school that I attended during my first pregnancy. I was in awe of the circles of my life. Here I was, back at this school, as a teacher. Back then, my regular high school would not let me attend while pregnant out of fear for my health and safety that far along in my pregnancy. So, they sent me to the Sussex Technical School District, a vocational and technical school, to continue my education in the evenings until my son was born that March. Six weeks later, I would resume my coursework at my regular high school and graduate with my class. After leaving that exit interview, I went home in that beautiful white stretch limousine and still, to this day, laugh about how life works in circles sometimes. It was the best exit interview in all of history.

I refused all offers to assist me with résumé writing and seeking job opportunities as well. I knew how to do all of these things well, and others needed this help more than I needed it. I made such an impression of how well I knew this stuff that I was offered an opportunity to assist dislocated workers in transitioning from the DuPont Nylon Plant in Seaford, Delaware. These dislocated workers were changing careers as that plant was downsizing. It seemed as though one door closed and many others began to open. I continued to seek higher education and eventually earned six education certifications ranging from Special Education to Administration of Grades 1–12. I had finally found something that I was passionate about. I loved teaching and mentoring young minds. The student population hadn't changed much since I was there, as many of them were in homes with poverty and abuse. Some of the students had learning disabilities, while others had severe mental issues and behavior problems. This required a certain type of teacher to work with them, and I was that person. From my first day as a substitute teacher to my last days in administration, my love for the hardest to love remained.

I didn't see these students as being so very different from other students. I had the same expectations of them as I did of any other student. For the most part, they lived up to my expectations. Because of the love I had for these students, the passion I had for teaching, and the fact that I could empathize with some of their issues, I received nice pay raises and was often recognized for my hard work. The school closed in the middle of June, five years later. But before it did, I was nominated as Teacher of the Year, for which I received many letters of endorsement for my skills.

I was then offered an opportunity to work in adult education. With the exception of my experience in teaching classes for dysfunctional juveniles, I didn't know if this job would be the right fit for me at first. As it turned out, it was for the same school I had attended for a few months of my senior year. It also required me to teach classes in the prison setting. I began teaching incarcerated females who wanted to acquire their GED and high school diplomas. Every year, I influenced at least thirty percent of my students to acquire the twenty-three essential credits to obtain their high school diploma. I did so well that I was transferred to the men's prison. I also became involved in the Delaware Adult Association of Community Education, or D.A.A.C.E, where I was quickly nominated to become president. I served as president for two years.

The outgoing President of D.A.A.C.E, Hazel Showell, asked me to pray for her one morning before she began the final meeting with her President's Address. I felt so humbled and privileged that my light was shining in such a place. It was Hazel who approached me to take her place. I served my two-year term in this position and, like Hazel, ended my term seeking a replacement to lead the next wave of change.

When the school for juveniles closed, I decided to apply for an internship as a UniServe director through the National Education Association. Their headquarters were located in Washington, D.C. I knew absolutely nothing about this type of work, but I had a desire to learn and to relocate. Thus I embarked on and entered yet another big undertaking and new organization. From day one, I felt uncomfortable during this training for this new career path. But however difficult "boot camp" was, I was determined to stick it out and see it through to the end.

The organization was tough for me as a forty-year-old in a career transition. Unbeknownst to me, they had already given out assignments and started the day before I showed up for training. So, when I arrived in my white Lexus in front of the hotel, I saw all the trainees in the lobby area. One of the leaders of the organization singled me out for arriving unprepared and a day late. I sat there composed as she lashed out at me. I remained polite and unrattled. One of the other trainees reached over to me at lunch and asked, "How did you manage to sit there and take the verbal attack?"

Smiling, I said, "Who do you remember from that conversation, me or her?"

I was always shining my light on the meanest of people. It was hard for me, coming from a management position, to sit in a room so cold you could see the steam coming off the coffee. They told me I had to change my hair color, so I bought a brunette wig to appease them. I told the girl living next to me when I came home one night I was going to quit. But thankfully, she encouraged me to hang in there. And I did achieve much success as a UniServe director.

Last but not least, one of the most important appointments I received was as a corporate board member of my church, Faith, Hope and Love Christian Fellowship. When my cousin Ralph became pastor and bishop of the church, it was an honor to step into the role he called me to fill. I assisted in completing the necessary paperwork for the church to become a 501c3 non-profit organization. As usual, I had neither experience nor understanding of this task. However, I accepted this challenge and was successful. Eventually, I was appointed as the church's business administrator.

Ralph had once told me I was just too humble. I looked at him astonished, unsure what he meant. He also told me once that there were people jealous of me. Given all I had been through, that was hard for me to see or understand. I believe that everyone has the same capability to achieve what I have in my life. Faith, determination, and hard work, along with God's grace and mercy, are the formula to success.

Throughout my church life, it has been stated many times that only what you do for Christ will stand. While I ended up retiring twice from full-time careers, I truly feel as though I have been serving the Lord faithfully in each one of them. My strong will, once viewed as a curse when I was growing up, became my biggest asset. Without strong willpower, there were many situations such as these I would never have survived.

The amazing common thread between most of these positions was that there was sometimes little pay. Instead, my hard work was rewarded with the joy of being able to help other people. I began to realize my calling in life was to help others. The crosses I learned to carry were heavy. Whether they were my burdens or the weight of someone else's, I didn't give up, no matter how hard it was to break through the barrier.

# Parenthood

*"Let us not become weary in doing good,*
*for at the proper time, we will reap a harvest*
*if we do not give up."*

Galatians 6:9 NIV

## Lakhira, Jermia, Jerrin, Jasmine, and Markell

Motherhood is something I knew I wanted from a young age, and it is one of the life accomplishments that I am most proud of. I used to commute forty-five miles to work daily, dropping my young sons off at the daycare halfway. I would be praying they didn't get sick during the day and need to be picked up. I worked my eight-hour shift, busting my butt to leave the office to start the forty-five-mile commute back home to get my children. I'd have to find a babysitter and turn around and drive over forty-five miles to attend evening classes at college for four hours. Then I would head back down the highway again to end the day. Once home, after making sure my sons were alright and tucked in bed, I would wash baby bottles and clothes, mix formula, and pack the children's bags so the next morning I could start this cycle over again and make it to work on time. Sometimes it would require speeding (as much as I tried to avoid it).

One morning, in my haste to drop the children off and get to work on time, I was driving my Volkswagen Beetle and slid into a barrier. After checking to make sure my children were unharmed, I continued my journey with a bent fender. I arrived a few minutes late that morning but walked into the office as though nothing had happened. I was just so grateful to God that I had traveling grace and mercy.

Sometime in my forties, I assumed guardianship of my grandchildren, Jasmine and her brother Jerrin. This was after my youngest son, their father, had something that kept him away for some years. The children's mother doesn't have a high school diploma, and you would know it if you met her. I finished raising the two of them along with two of their older half-sisters (each of whom had different mothers). My house was crazy for a while, with three teenage girls and one teenage boy. Despite the constant commotion, it comforted me like memories of my own childhood living with extended family and cousins.

Lakhira, Jermia, Jerrin, and Jasmine fought and argued almost every day.

Jerrin Jr. was more disciplined than his three sisters. He looked a lot like his dad. He had, however, dark brown skin and a mischievous grin. Honestly, it's amazing I still have hair on my head (albeit some gray now from his antics). He lived like a tornado had touched down, with stinky clothes piled in his room, muddled with a mix of trash or dirty dishes. He even punched many holes in my walls and a brand-new flatscreen television. Under the bed were empty alcohol bottles and used cigarette butts. I was at the end of my rope, but I spent every dollar I had to redo a shed so he could live independently. Everywhere I placed him on my property, he was destined to destroy it.

But even after I would drop him off at the treatment center, he would come out laughing. I did what any grandmother would do and helped the best I could. After buying him two cars, paying his auto insurance, paying a lawyer two thousand dollars to keep a DUI off his record, and keeping him out of prison, I finally had enough. I could cry quite a bit when it came time to send this young man to a shelter to live; he was fully grown but very immature. I was concerned that he would bring harm to himself or someone else, and we all know that society identifies with situations like this, but we talk more than we do. We had multiple conversations about him needing to grow up, but each time, we fell into a cycle of codependency.

I had him placed in a vacant mobile home rental to avoid sending someone as destructive as he was to a shelter. But during Labor Day weekend, he was taken to a shelter in Wilmington, Delaware. He stayed in the shelter for a few days before contacting me with crocodile tears. He called on a Sunday morning around four a.m., saying the shelter was making everyone get out at six a.m. He said they didn't care where you went, but you had to get out of the center so they could clean it and prepare meals, etc. Needless to say, having worked in the Wilmington area in the prison system for several years, I knew he wouldn't make it at the shelter or on the streets. He wasn't streetwise. So when he called, although he had done so much wrong by me, I drove two hours away to pick this young man up.

On the two-hour ride back downstate, I was in a rush to get back home to get myself and my elderly mother showered and ready for church. Jerrin claimed to be starving, so I stopped by a WaWa gas station and gave him money to get a breakfast sandwich. When he came out, he apologized for spending some of my change on a pack of cigarettes. He was always doing things like this, manipulating money out of people or getting them to do whatever he wanted. Once he tricked me into buying him an Xbox, which, after I'd stood in line on Black Friday to buy him one, he then sold for fifty dollars because he claimed he "needed money in his pocket." What's worse, he pulled the same antics twice more, and each time, I felt gullible to his selfish charm. He refused medication and employment opportunities, each time coming back to me to remedy his victimhood.

It would never end as long as I continued being suckered in and feeling sorry for him. In his mind, the world was wrong and against him. In a way, I empathized too deeply, but my empathy was causing me to suffer. I finally decided to show him some tough love. I could no longer stay up after midnight to pick him up from work, take care of my elderly mother, and drag him back to work in the evenings. I ended up making a call to a strong male friend who was able to physically remove him from my property and get him into a shelter.

Of course, I wasn't sure if I made the right decision by him. As I began to second-guess, God reminded me I had turned this over to him. I needed to trust Him with Jerrin's care, as I had with Jerrin Sr.'s incarceration. I had to let God work it out. Because sometimes the only thing we have for comfort is faith.

His sister, Jasmine, is extremely intelligent. She managed to graduate high school a year early with honors, no less. However, Jasmine lacked common sense. She ended up pregnant after graduation. I remember her morning sickness was so bad that she asked me to take her to the hospital, thinking they would be able to give her something to feel better. I declined and explained it was normal, which only made her upset. She asked her older sister to take her instead. Before she left my driveway, screaming and cursing at me, she threw a large wooden hairbrush at the house, which broke a window. At eighteen years old, she went on to have a healthy baby, whom she named Milani.

When Milani was six months old, Jasmine once again had a conflict in the driveway. She was carrying her in the baby carrier with one arm when Milani was dropped on the concrete. Jasmine screamed at the top of her voice for me to come. As fast as I could, I grabbed my car keys and put on my flashers. We were at the hospital in fewer than fifteen minutes. Some paramedics overheard my explanation and assisted in moving the bystanders out of the way so that we could get this baby immediate help. The doctors, thank God, determined everything was alright. I cried and praised heaven for this miracle.

My mother, who was at the time quite elderly, quickly grew attached to this baby. But Milani was taken away from us when Jasmine moved to Dover. Jasmine started living in a motel, which I paid over a hundred dollars a night just to keep them off the street or keep them from sleeping in cars. Eventually, the motel refused to accept my money as they were too long-term. I ended up renting her and her boyfriend an apartment in my name. I later found out that her sorry boyfriend also told his drug-addicted mother, his sister, and her boyfriend, along with the sister's three babies, to move in with them. This was all at my expense. The landlord evicted all of them because of frequent police calls to the property. Thankfully, before the eviction, I had made a visit to serve notice and said that I wasn't paying another dime for them to live on. This protected me from any legal action.

Not only did I specialize in spoiling and enabling Jerrin and Jasmine, but they have two other siblings that I did the same (or worse) to. Jermia, the one I named, ironically looked much like me. She was extremely pretty and, on my part, pathetically spoiled. As a child, she didn't want anyone to sit next to me but her. When she was younger, she lived with her mother about forty-five minutes away and would call me every weekend. On the weekends, I would have her; I would take her to the stores to buy whatever she wanted. I would then order out from an expensive seafood establishment to get her a pound or so of snow crab legs. When she became a teenager, she began to have conflicts with her mother and thus came to live with me. She graduated from high school and enrolled in junior college, but her behavior never changed.

It wasn't long before she decided to become a certified nurse practitioner. Although she worked hard to achieve this, she met who she thought was the love of her life. She became pregnant. I was on my way home from work when she called me crying to break the news. I had, throughout their lives, explained to them how to avoid raising children while they were still children themselves. I encouraged them to establish careers and further their education goals before becoming parents. In all this, she felt she had disappointed me. I consoled her by telling her I had conceived my first child when I was seventeen. I assured her it would be alright and that she could still do positive things with her life.

She developed into a caring, responsible mother to a daughter she named Kali. I'm sure that both she and Jasmine realized their lives were going to be different after giving birth to these beautiful little girls. Both Jasmine and Jermia saw a difference with their babies' fathers after they gave them their bodies. I had always cautioned them that sex never necessarily kept a man. Sex sometimes creates more issues in a relationship.

I explained how it is not a positive experience for the child if there are co-parenting issues. Long term, in most instances, the consequences can create ill feelings among young parents as they struggle to positively and appropriately raise their children. I was not fortunate to have grown up in a normal family unit—consisting of a mother and father together to raise children. Despite the battles early on with their children's fathers, both Jasmine and Jermia have smoothed out the relationships enough to co-parent.

As I write, Jermia is very close to obtaining her degree and has recently purchased a home. Jasmine has found her own housing and is making positive strides to continue her education, majoring in Human Services at Delaware State University.

Lakhira, who is older than Jasmine and Jermia, waited a little longer to become pregnant. It was no piece of cake raising her either, as she was very rebellious and made some mistakes that could have been very costly. On one occasion, she decided to leave my home after we had a verbal altercation. I didn't agree with her decision, but she was of age, and so she left. As she moved out, I thought about all the times I had transported her to the schools of her choice, speeding to not be late for work after dropping her off and in the evenings to pick her up when school ended.

But she was ambitious, and so I sacrificed to assist in paying her tuition to cosmetology school. When she was within six months of completing the program, she decided she could not finish because she couldn't take the chemical smell in the salon. I was extremely disappointed but had to accept the mistake I knew she was making. No matter how I tried to encourage her otherwise, she had made up her mind, and I wouldn't change it.

After some hesitancy, she did marry her baby's father. They are doing a wonderful job raising this super intelligent and jovial youngster they named Camryn. Lakhira is now enrolled in studies to become a dental hygienist and has almost completed those studies. I am sure she will excel in that, with her beautiful teeth and a warm, room-lighting smile.

Finally, there is Markell. He is the latest to join the family. No one, except my son Jerrin, knew anything about Markell. He had attempted to contact Jerrin but had no luck. It was Jasmine who first came across Markell, who, through Facebook, reached out to his father. After they met in person, Jasmine came by my house to tell me how much Markell looked like their dad, Jerrin Sr. I was very anxious to meet Markell, who was residing in Cape Charles, Virginia, at the time. I arranged to meet him the immediate Sunday after church. I didn't hesitate, but he did. He was uncertain how he would be received by our family. But I assured him we had nothing but love waiting for him.

So after church, I drove to Cape Charles, where he met me along with his adorable, then one-year-old twin boys. I was accompanied by my mother and Kira, who was also anxious to meet this younger brother. When Markell came into the restaurant, I noted that he was a handsome young man. He had a baby carrier in each arm, looking almost identical to his father. He was thinner than his dad but had his father's smile. I immediately embraced him and called him my grandson.

We got better acquainted over a meal, catching up on twenty-three years in only a couple of hours. The irony is that despite having just met him, I saw he definitely has my personality. I later realized that, like me, he had grown up longing to have a more wholesome family dynamic. We were shocked to find that Markell rode the same bus as his younger sister and brother, Jasmine and Jerrin, for years. He rode past my house daily and could describe seeing my little black sports car in the driveway. He also informed me he lived less than a half-mile from my house, although he never made contact with me. The family he had always wanted and was already his was living right down the road.

After a while, the babies started to become anxious. Auntie Lakhira took the new nephews in her arms and laid them on her chest. One decided to fall asleep. The afternoon had gone so well that none of us wanted to go home. Before we left, we took pictures and made plans for Markell and Shayniece, his fiancé, to come and visit in the very near future. Now that we knew each other, there was a lot of catching up to do.

Markell made good on his promise, and by late summer, he had come to visit. He went to church with us, and of course, everybody looked at me like I had six heads. I had been through so much with all the other grandkids. But I was so excited to get close to this newly found grandchild. It was neither his fault nor mine that we didn't know each other. However, when God deemed it the appropriate time, we did meet.

Along on the visit with Markell were his fiancé, Shayniece, and the adorable twin boys. These little boys were precious and had developed their own personalities. They refused to go to sleep in my house, which was a new environment for them. We tried everything and, by the end, were so tired that by the time we left for dinner the next day, the twins finally slept. We enjoyed a wonderful meal at Matt's Seafood in Rehoboth, which is only about fifteen minutes from my home. We then came back to my house. We sat on the porch, laughing and enjoying ourselves.

It was still hard to believe I was meeting this grandson for the first time. He was very responsible, unlike a couple of his siblings that I had raised. He has stability in a job at a brewery where he has been working for over three years. Since the first day of the face-to-face meeting with Markell, there haven't been many days that we haven't video chatted through FaceTime or talked on the phone. One of his twin boys looks almost identical to Jerrin Sr., and the younger of the twins looks like my other son, Jevon. It was almost like watching my sons grow up again.

My middle son, Jevon, has given me two grandchildren. He and his wife do quite well in life, and the children are straight-A students in school. At present, one is entering the sixth grade, and the other one is going to enter the ninth grade this fall. They also do well in sports, playing baseball, softball, wrestling, football, and soccer. My grandson must have fifty wrestling trophies. I am grateful and proud of these grandchildren. I'm also grateful and proud of the wonderful parents my son and my daughter-in-law are. I see them sacrificing time, energy, and finances in order for these children to excel.

In my mind, life doesn't always seem or appear perfect, but it is fair; despite what we think, the divine plan always works better than what we could imagine for our lives. Parenting meant sacrifices. Parenting was a continuation of my employment as an educator. Parenting meant I had to lead by example and show the importance of having good sense. In life, we don't learn it all in school. We just do the best we can in any situation. Many people have asked me why I didn't just give up on them. But God does not give up on people.

And so I can't give up on them. My ex-husband used to say that I have too much patience. I'm always looking for the good in every person. Because God doesn't make junk, I guess it was just out of love that I did so much for my family. I didn't want any child to have to go through what I went through. These children had my blood. And I trust that God has a plan even in the messiness. I believe that's what is meant when the Lord says to lean not on your own understanding (Proverbs 3:5–6). I am a mom. I am a grandmom. I am a superwoman.

Jaylen & Jace

It has been stated that no two people see a rainbow in the sky exactly the same way. That is because rainbows are unique to individuals. I was leaving the YMCA recently and saw not one but two rainbows in the sky. Very excited, I immediately opened my phone and took pictures of the double rainbows. I began to feel a sense of gratitude and was also reminded that rainbows show up to remind us of God's promise. The gratitude within me grew at the thought of all the promises God has made me, promises He has always kept.

Two of my grandchildren are a representation of those rainbows. My son Jevon and his wife Beth have cultivated all the qualities and meanings of rainbows in them. After having gone through so much in my life, I am now realizing God is yet again giving me double for my past troubles.

Jevon and Beth's daughter, Jaylen, has been a straight-A student since she first began school; I attribute her success to the parental sacrifices made by Jevon and Beth. On her own, however, she studies difficult subject matters along the way, and she has worked hard to maintain the highest grades. During the height of the COVID-19 pandemic, she faced the interruption to her schooling with great grace. She earned her acceptance to highly sought-after schools in Virginia by interviewing well, presenting herself with poise, and exhibiting her talent and capabilities. She is now a sophomore and still maintaining her scholastic achievement. Jaylen has not only excelled academically but has also received many awards. She works hard physically and rises to the top in athletics, being especially gifted in softball. I have no doubt she will reach her goal of becoming a doctor or lawyer as she continues on life's journey, putting God first.

Jace is my other rainbow. He is doing exceptionally well and continues to excel in all areas of life. He too has been a straight-A student throughout his entire education process. I call him my gentle giant (most of the time). He is easygoing but proves to be strong in academics and sports. Jace started playing ball with individuals three and four years his senior. Although he was smaller in stature, I wouldn't have known he was younger than the others. This is because he played so well and displayed such mature sportsmanship. Although he had a mishap that caused him to have surgery twice in the last few years, he still continues to win championships in wrestling and football, even with the pins in his arm. His room is filled with all the trophies he earns.

For these rainbows in my life, I am grateful. They work extremely hard along with the love and support of their parents, who are positive role models for them. Although my son came from a dysfunctional home, Jevon rose above it and broke that cycle with his children and family. These two youngest grandchildren have helped me to remember that God has not forgotten us. He has heard every prayer and has felt every tear. I am grateful.

I thank God for the rainbows and the promises my grandchildren represent:

RED – They exhibit strong emotions as well as wisdom. They also demonstrate vitality and enthusiasm.

ORANGE – They are both warm and happy. They are creative and enjoy life. They are strong and possess endurance.

YELLOW – They think and communicate effectively. They are cheerful and orderly.

GREEN – They represent good health and show growth in all areas of their lives through their achievements and accomplishments.

BLUE – They have stability as well as trust and loyalty. They demonstrate care for others and treat them with respect. They hold each other accountable. Blue also represents their strong spiritual connections.

INDIGO – They both show creativity and imagination in their abilities to perform academically and athletically.

# Mercy

*"He kept me from going to the world of the dead,*
*and I am still alive."*

Job 33:28 GNT

Upon having started writing this book, I would've thought my story was close to done. That the years ahead were going to be less eventful than the years behind. But in 2021, during a global pandemic, I found my story once again starting to unravel. This time, I had been quarantined for weeks because of COVID pneumonia. In order to prevent myself from spreading the disease, I allowed more than adequate quarantine time. The whole world was shut down, and everyone was concerned for their lives and the lives of their loved ones. After all I've gone through, I can't take any chances, especially given my lungs were compromised because of my respiratory ailments. So, for much of January 2021, I had been recuperating after being hospitalized, fighting to get my lungs breathing and energy level back, even learning to walk again.

Without God's help, I couldn't see the world getting through this period, let alone myself isolated in a room. After several months of rest and isolation, I was feeling better and allowed myself to venture back into my life outside my bedroom. A knock came on the door.

"It's me, Mom. I wanted to surprise you by coming by to watch the football game with you," I heard a familiar voice say. The surprise visitor made me extremely happy, and it felt like old times again.

John is my first son, named after his father. He has a minor in biology and studied science. He has called this pandemic step by step since the beginning. He began gathering supplies and food in the early days to prepare for quarantine when everyone thought he was overreacting. Turns out he was right on. In the two months prior to March 2020, he warned me and his fellow teachers what we were in for. He self-quarantined immediately and urged others to wear masks, as did I, along with other family members and friends.

My son John made sure I had everything I needed or wanted. It was he who drove me to the hospital when I first contracted the virus. I had never seen him so scared, this being the first time in his life he had ever seen me horribly sick. As he drove me to the hospital, I could see him peer over at me, fear in his eyes. He later told me he worried that was going to be the last time he saw his mother alive. All I could do was lay my head back and close my eyes as I struggled to breathe. When I finally arrived at the hospital, I couldn't muster up enough energy to walk inside. They brought me a wheelchair that I slid into as I waited for the next directive. I was given a room, and with me lying on the stretcher, they immediately began critical care. They told John that he should check back in three hours, but from my symptoms, they were almost certain it was COVID-19.

At this point, I wasn't listening or aware of what was being said. I could feel myself drifting in and out of consciousness. I do remember the doctors surrounding me, looking down like Martians in some sci-fi film, explaining to me what they were doing. They were all in those yellow and white disposable suits to protect themselves from contracting the virus. They were covered head to toe: headgear as well as face shields. I suppose I looked frightened as the doctor approached me and began to introduce himself. The doctor pulled out his identification badge that indeed read, "Dr. Art." He then tried to convince me that I was in capable hands. I wanted to believe they were going to take care of me and help me feel better. I was too out of it to remember anything past this point other than fear and sickness.

They began giving me blood pressure medicine, though I assured them I only took natural medication daily and that it had been working fine for me. I spent five hours in the Emergency Care unit as they continued to ask a barrage of questions: Who lived in the house with me? Where did I contract the sickness? What symptoms did I have?

But COVID brain fog had already set in, robbing me of my memory. Trying to dictate my wishes became more and more difficult. I asked my son to stop at the grocery store to pick up the store-brand Very Cherry fruit cocktail. When he returned, he got everything I'd asked for from the store but forgot the fruit cocktail.

"So, I'm the one who has COVID brain fog, huh?" I said.

He sprinted back to the store, and I texted him to apologize. We had a good laugh about that.

One thing that stands out from this time was a dispute between John and his younger brother, Jevon. John and Jevon, who ranks high in the career path with our government as a federal agent, often had a clash of opinions regarding coronavirus. There appears to be even a bit of a political undertone in these disagreements. I wasn't accepting any excuses. I told them they had better put their differences aside, and they'd better do it today. We sat on the phone one evening, and I had afforded each one time to explain their side of the issue. When all was said and done, I prayed for divine guidance for each of them. In less than a week, the older one called to say they had resolved the issue, and they were getting along as if nothing had happened. They might not always agree because they are individuals, but the fact still remains they are brothers. Besides, I was going to need them both weeks later when times got hard for me.

In the hospital, during those isolated months of recovery, I called my sister, Brenda, to discuss my elderly mother's placement. Brenda, with health struggles of her own, couldn't agree to take on our mother's care. She was at the casino during the call. I could hear the machines whirling in the background, making me wonder if she was really as sick as she claimed she was. I now know that she was dealing with a lot. Before I retired, I had started taking extra care for my mother. I moved her in with me a few years after retiring— meaning I had spent seven years total providing her care.

"I'm not going to no d*** nursing home," Mom said before we decided that was indeed what was best for both of our health. Then she became the chatterbox of the nursing home (so much so that she had to be moved from room to room).

Prior to moving Mom to the nursing home, I said, "Good night, Mom," one night after I had moved her into my house.

"It's a good night for you. You're in your own house." I could hear the anguish in her voice.

I had to stop myself from snapping back and instead gracefully said, "You had seven children, and it looks like I'm the only one here to take care of you."

She got quiet and didn't make a grumble or complaint after that. But I could see it was hard for her to relinquish the independence she craved when she needed so much support. She could no longer cook her chicken 'n dumplin' dish or famous dinner rolls. It was me and her now. Throughout the whole process of care, I was there to pick her up from the hospital, even in the pouring rain, with no one there to assist.

The trouble with having these conversations with Brenda about our mother was that I too was still in need of care. They would call me in my hospital bed, laid up ill, to ask if Mom could be transferred to this nursing home or that hospital. I was so weak that I couldn't even dictate information when my son would come to visit me, much less on behalf of my elderly mother, who had two strokes and dementia. I didn't want her to be put at risk by exposure to the virus. Surprisingly, my sister and I came to a decent conclusion.

I believe when I can't handle things, I give it to God, and He works it out.

We didn't have much of a problem during childhood, Brenda and I, because we'd only spent a week together during the summer. After we had discussed our mother's care, we began to talk about our different fathers and brothers. Our brothers were always masking their substance use with their perception of a terrible childhood. This was their excuse for indulging in substance(s). But through this conversation with Brenda, it became clear that she and I shared a horrible secret. She brought up a cousin of ours, and there was a tremble in her voice as she recalled the terror that stole her innocence.

She looked me in my eyes and said, "Right in the house that you're living in, the same thing happened to me by one of our cousins. Didn't you notice how he would always say how pretty I am?"

Brenda went on to share with me that when she was twelve years old, she had been molested in our grandparents' house—the house I had now remodeled and now live in. She never told my mother or anyone about the experience. My mother's husband, our stepfather, used to come into her bedroom when she was very young, and she'd wake up to find him standing over her. This is the same man who would hit her with a two-by-four because she refused to eat what he had cooked. She told me that she blocked it out of her mind, which is how she kept her sanity. That worked for her for a while, she said, until a partner she was seeing tried to touch her when she was asleep. Her reaction was so strong that it brought up the unpleasant memories of the rape.

My reply to this was to share with her how I had to ask God to help me and forgive my abusers. It took me a long time to get to a place where I considered forgiveness. Coley Sr. had made it so difficult for me in a lot of ways, but ultimately, it was hardest for me to really love others and receive love. He would tell me he loved me, but I knew this inappropriate behavior between an adult and a child, no less supposedly a father and a daughter, was not love.

Like my sister, I didn't know who to tell. Especially since Betty also hated me for looking like my mother. Her abuse was of the violent variety, beating me unmercifully every day with blunt objects or her fists. Sometimes she would beat me so hard I would begin to see stars or harbor long bruises for weeks on my body. I could not so much as mumble or sigh a cry. I felt as though nothing (and I mean nothing) could surpass what I had lived through. By talking to my sister, I was able to finally unburden myself to someone who maybe understood.

Many people who have expired and are no longer with us had contracted COVID-19. But the pandemic was the start of my healing within my family. No matter what I've been through, I still feel blessed to be here and alive to tell the story. And I thank God constantly for bringing me through. Of all those who took the role of the abuser, God knows exactly who and what they really are. Many years passed, and I continued searching for answers to these simple but deeply complex questions. Why had we been abandoned? What kind of God would allow for a world to be overtaken by a sickness or plague? Did anybody really see or care for us? I know now that sometimes the help or angels we need are within our own families. All I needed to do was reach out for help.

# Forgiveness

*"Forgive anyone who has caused you pain or harm.*
*Keep in mind that forgiving is not for others.*
*It is for you. Forgiving is not forgetting.*
*It is remembering without anger.*
*It frees up your power and heals*
*your body, mind, and spirit.*
*Forgiveness opens up a pathway*
*to a new place of peace where you can*
*persist despite what has happened to you."*

—Les Brown

Death helps us prioritize or evaluate the severity of the anguish of life. In my life, I can say I have had many hurt feelings and probably have hurt a few too. In the end, we all wonder, "Can I cross over?"

We say we forgive, but is it lip service, or is it real? I have been wronged by so many people, and to reach a place where I can't even remember what they did to me has been a long journey. And it's not just because I'm older. It's because God really did wipe the slate clean. For me to say that I hold no hard feelings against any of the people I have mentioned in this book is nothing short of heaven's miraculous power.

Betty passed about three years before her husband, Coley Sr., died. Betty passed away in a nursing home in Boston when she became oxygen-deprived. Of course, my mind wondered whether someone in the nursing home had become angry enough to cover her oxygen tube. After all, she continued to rub people the wrong way, even to the end. Dementia can bring out the evilest emotions. When Betty's death came, I saddled up with two of my cousins and my partner at that time and went to the funeral. Now, being completely honest, my purpose in going to this funeral was to make sure this woman was dead and buried deep. I wanted to make sure she could not bring any harm to anyone else.

My brother Coley Jr. refused to go to the funeral. I am not surprised, as he had to be begged one Father's Day to accompany me back to Boston to visit ailing Coley Sr. I tried explaining to him that his father, whom he was named after, was nearing the end of his life. He looked at me on church grounds as we stood outside after church, dismissing the idea with sadness in his eyes. "Don't you know they were trying to murder us?" Coley Jr. said.

I told him I was so busy just trying to survive. I'm sad to say he was proven right. After Coley Sr. passed away, the children they raised went to clean up the apartment. Jerry, the baby cousin I helped raise, found insurance policies for all of us. We were worth more to them dead than we were alive.

As I sat there amongst the modest crowd at Betty's funeral, I couldn't wrap my head around who they were talking about. The flowery send-off definitely didn't describe the woman my brother and I knew. They made her sound like a halfway-decent human being who did good in this world for others. I knew this woman was a different story.

Once again, I reflect on when I went to Boston when Betty passed away. I was driving from Delaware to Boston to pay respect to this woman who had made life a nightmare for my brother and me. I had always said that I wasn't worried about going to hell because I was living in hell.

One of my cousins pointed to the obituary I was holding. They noted that neither my brother nor I were included in the survivors. I told them that I was fine with that. They remained upset and were determined to speak to their uncle about it. After all, my brother was named after this man.

I said it was excusable given that Coley Sr. only had a second-grade education, thereby not realizing the error. Or maybe somewhere in his cruel heart he was deeply upset at the loss of his wife of over fifty-nine years and overlooked the matter.

As I sat in that service reading Betty's obituary to hide my eyes from scanning the room, new revelations and truth gleamed. In the same obituary, I noticed some crossover in the dates that sent my mind into a frenzy of revelation. My mother was fifteen years old when my brother Coley was born. Almost exactly four months after giving birth to my brother Coley, she became pregnant with me ... at the same time, Betty and Coley married one another.

The way we ended up with these individuals was because of the squabbles of young love. Coley Sr. had come from North Carolina to Delaware because he had family there and felt he could make more money, doing better for himself by moving north. He met my mother, Frances, and sweet-talked her into getting involved with him. This meant my mother was only fourteen years old when she became pregnant, at a time when Coley Sr. was, of course, sowing his wild oats and had no intention of marrying her. It was at the same time that he met Betty.

Betty, I discovered, had left her abusive father's house at eighteen years old, completing the eighth grade and knowing nothing about life, let alone knowing anything about men. In the midst of this love triangle, they all ended up attending the same church, the church my grandmother and grandfather had taken my mother to since she was in the womb. My grandfather and the pastor were closer than brothers. I have been told my grandfather helped build the church.

I know he was the oldest deacon in the church. This meant he had strict expectations for his family.

This was the source of the huge falling out and the start of the troubles for Coley Jr. and me, two young innocent children. It was exactly three months after all this that my mother gave birth to me and that Coley Sr. and Betty decided to marry. I imagine my mother was severely hurt by their actions, having two children by a man who chose to marry someone else. She had come from a strict Christian home. I imagined my mother shamefully carrying around a toddler and a three-month-old little girl. She was all of sixteen years old, a baby herself. This could not have been easy.

Suddenly, at that moment, I realized how we ended up with this mean, near-crazy couple. What stood out to me from this obituary was the timeline. It hit me right in the face, the thing I'd never seen or known. *I WAS THE CHILD NOBODY WANTED.* My mother didn't want to be pregnant, and she had lost the man she loved to another woman. And Coley Sr., we know, didn't want any children at all.

So my mother and Betty were at odds from the beginning. And it was in the midst of this that I was born.

But for a split moment, I realized this was not easy for Betty either, knowing that my mother loved her husband and that they had two children together. Even if Coley Sr. had not married Betty, and Betty never wanted children, it must have still stung, knowing that he had at one point loved my mother and had children by my mother.

Years later, I came across Betty's diary. For the second time, I realized just how hurt this poor woman had been and felt empathy for the horrors that made her so mean in the first place. Her origin story was just as painful as mine had been.

# EXCERPTS FROM BETTY'S DIARY

We went to school and back home.
but the Lord bles all to graduate from
eigth grade unto the nineth grade.
but he would not us go farther.
My teacher beg him to let me go on.
but he wouldn't allow me to do it.
I was hurt unhappy Anger.
and that cause pain. I didn't have no
mother to help me.
I lost my Self Esteem. you might asked
what is Self Esteem.
It is her over all judgement of her self.
I love school. but Wasn't allowed to
finish school.
We never got encouragement
we was very hurt annoyed and wanting
to fight back at the peron that hurt us
but we dare to try.

What is Self esteem?
It is over all judgement of himself.
Conceit is to cover up low Self Esteem.
A child judgement of him self influence
the kinds of friends he chooses.
how he or she gets along with others.

Strugglion How To over come Pain Hurt and
be lonely with out a Mother
AT young Age. When you don't understand
why.

I was born in Lincoln Delaware
A child born unto Laura my mother and
James my father.
I understand my mother was mother
of 12 children. She must loss the other
3, before I knew them. or before I was
born. I only had the previlge to know
eight. I was the fifth of the other eight.

I can remmber the after noon
that one of my fathers friend came
to our house to tell my father that my
mother was ready to come home from the
hospital. because we didn't have know telephone
my father was down at the next farm
working. One of us went to tell him
but he didn't come home untill night.
they had to finish what they was doing.
and by the time he got ready to go get
her, the same man came back and said
she had died. So you can image the
hurt that came to him, and the
rest of us.
✦ We remmber the night that our mother
left home going to the hospital. Some of
us were younger than the others. It was
four older then me. I was the fifth child.
and it was four younger then me.
So my father was left looking for help
and didn't know how to find it. he
✦ wasn't a christian.
He was felling the pain of Lost.
Pain of fear. Pain of hurt. When he
wonder how he was going to take care
of nine children, who had loss their mother.
We would be looking for our mother when
◑ we left to go to school, and when we came home.
but she wasn't there any more.

Coley Sr. lasted for about three years after Betty passed. He ended up in a nice nursing home initially but was transferred to a deplorable one, where he ended up passing away. He had many surgeries before he died. The most painful thing was to watch as every organ in his body shut down. He requested to die naturally (by which I believe he meant not to be placed on life support). One of the young ladies raised by him and Betty was made his proxy, and she carried out this mission to the letter.

Arriving in Boston to visit Coley Sr. was different this time compared to many previous trips. I had been told he had stopped eating and was waiting to see me. It seemed to me that my brother, however, had no problem separating himself from my mother and our other siblings, as well as separating himself from his father. Prior to this last trip to Boston, a strange thing happened. The two Coleys did not recognize each other. Finally, though, on this trip, as we came face-to-face with Coley Sr., I asked if he knew who the man before him was, and he replied he had no idea. Now, at that time, Coley Sr. was still driving a car. He didn't have dementia.

"Are you serious?" I asked. "Yes," said Coley Sr.

As much as they looked alike, I could see the sincerity in his fading eyes. He didn't know his own son. I had to formally introduce them. I said, "Coley Sr., meet Coley Jr." I gave the same introduction to my brother; this would be the last time Coley Jr. would see him alive.

I continued to go back-and-forth to Boston. I wanted to give Coley Sr. a chance to say he was sorry; that never happened, but he said he was sorry to God. I hope that's what really mattered on my last trip to Boston before his passing. I decided to tell him that I had forgiven him before I left Boston that Saturday afternoon to head back to Delaware. I looked down at this man as I rubbed his forehead and told him I had forgiven him.

"Go ahead and cross over. I'll see you on the other side," I said to Coley Sr.

I had him repeat the Sinner's Prayer around midnight, knowing that death was coming soon. Therefore, I believe he made it into heaven in his final hours, for he was too ill to cause anyone any further harm. I made it back home to Delaware, got up that Sunday morning, and went to church. When I returned home, I got a call around four o'clock to say he had passed.

At the time of writing this, Brenda is fighting to live, recuperating from open-heart surgery. I have gone to Georgia multiple times and talked to doctors, nurses, hospital staff, and rehabilitation personnel, trying to assist my sister in any way I can. The family should always look out for the family. Of course, I'm talked about; many people shake their heads because I continually make sacrifices and go the extra mile for those who have hurt me. I really don't care what people say or do. I have to love everybody and help the best I can. After all, "Vengeance is mine," says the Lord. We have to walk as well as talk about the good life, aiming to please God rather than people and ourselves. That's where the rubber meets the road.

Coley Jr. continues fighting a rare cancer. He has been through so much but continues to weather the storms with strength and perseverance. He has bravely taken every treatment in the last few years, including all chemo-therapies and radiation. He has been a fighter and has depended on the Lord in this tough battle. He continues to improve because of God, and for that, I'm so grateful. My brother has been a good leader and inspiration to these fine groups of grandchildren, inspiring many of them to serve in the military, just as he had served. He does a lot for his church as well as other agencies in life. Out of all my siblings, we've been through so much together. Coley has been and always will remain a special brother to me. I started out referencing his faith, encouraging him to fight his cancer battle.

About two weeks ago from writing this, I buried my only husband of many years. In his mind, we were still married until one of us died. I often told him how fortunate he was that some men would give their right arm to have one son. I had given him three, and he was not appreciative or grateful enough to put them first or spend time with them. That I could never understand. It was all about him and his substances. He said once, "I'm going to take drugs until I die." And that's exactly what he did, although, in the end, they were prescribed and administered by the doctors.

He wasn't the best father and definitely wasn't much after the divorce. In the end, I couldn't receive benefits from the military because I chose to leave by divorce. I valued my life and my children's lives more than anything in this world. He took on his girlfriend's family and did virtually nothing for his own children. He didn't have to pay child support.

As I looked down at the remains of this once six-foot-three-inch man weighing more than 240 pounds (who now had shrunk to under six feet weighing fewer than 175 pounds), I could only imagine the hurt my sons must've been feeling as they assisted in covering this. I watched our sons secure the coffin, with my assistance, of a man who chose to do so little for them throughout their lives. In the end, his neglect resulted in letting the property, our marriage, and his relationship with his children go to nothing. His self-neglect had finally done him in too.

At my husband's funeral, I said, "Forgiveness is not about the other person. It is about you. You must be forgiving in order to be forgiven. Live each day to the fullest as if there is no tomorrow. Step two is to forgive everyone. Know you can't do it by yourself. But know that God's grace is sufficient. Step three is to love everybody. This is the commandment you can keep with God's help."

These steps, I've learned in life, are the hardest to follow. Who can forgive a man like Coley Sr. or John? Who can forgive someone like Betty? But it's necessary to forgive, so I do. It is not just lip service.

John finally got it right before he left this earth and was baptized, declaring Jesus as his personal Lord and Savior. For this, I was happy. As I did with Coley Sr., I told John I forgave him for everything. I told John I loved him. Turns out John had confessed to our oldest son, who was named after him. He told him that he was sorry for how he treated me because I was a good woman. He was very sorry for leaving his family. Our son John was there for him to the very end, despite how he had treated him.

I suppose, in some ways, I had finally begun to understand too that he was only perpetuating the cycle of pain we had both experienced in our youth. And as the saying goes, hurt people often hurt other people. He too suffered in the end and paid an AWFUL price in his slow death. Hopefully, he's at peace now. For that peace, I thank God.

At this point in life, all my aunts and uncles, save my mother's one sister, Aunt Lydia, and her one brother, Uncle George, have passed. All of those who have abused me are all deceased. They say hurt people hurt people, and again, that's exactly what it was for most of my caretakers. But I am a testament that it does not always have to result in a domino cycle of hurt. The cycle can be broken by those who are brave and forgiving enough to live life differently.

I consider myself a miracle.

# *Acknowledgments*

## December 17, 2022

This book is written to help individuals sharing some of these same experiences, feeling like they are hopeless misfits in life. Also, it is hoped that this book will inspire many individuals struggling to reach their full potential against a world of obstacles. Domestic violence is not your fate. It is my hope that after reading this book, you will be able to catch a second wind and grab hold of your faith. Believe all things really are possible. May you find purpose in life and see your dreams realized as you continue to strive for your prize in life.

As I bring closure to my book, I have pondered which way to leave you, the reader. The inspiration came as usual for me at about three or four in the morning. That is when my best revelations come to my mind. As I typed, I prayed that I could put on paper what had surfaced. The overwhelming fact of my life has been that despite the negative experiences, I have gained many positive things. The first reason my life has turned out for the better is because I was able to truly forgive. And I was not just saying it, but by my God-given strength, I was able to forgive those who harmed me. But forgiveness has its own timeline. Many people will say that they're "not there yet" when it comes to forgiving their offenders. They may say that they "couldn't" or "can't" forgive others. But the secret is that you, of yourself, cannot forgive with any significant magnitude. It's not possible to flippantly forgive after many decades and many instances of repeated abuse.

However, when we are spiritually grounded, rooted so deeply in the love of God, we realize that both our blessings and success stop when there is unforgiveness within us. It is simply a no-brainer. In order to forgive, we must then ask the Creator to help us to forgive everyone for everything. I asked for not only grace and mercy but blessings too for those who had wronged me. I do this every time a situation or memory arises that requires it. I have not been, nor will I ever be, perfect. If we want to be forgiven for our imperfections and shortcomings, we must remember that we cannot receive what we do not give to others. This lesson is something that I've drilled into my sons and countless others. And while I do not know your personal situation, I can only tell you what has worked (and continues to work) for me. I offer you to give it a try with a guarantee that it will cost you nothing and gain you everything.

—————————————∽∞∾—————————————

As for my family mentioned in the book, they are well.

My firstborn son, John, remains a bachelor, although he is very handsome and intelligent. He remains close and has visited the young people who took him as a mentor. He is a wonderful role model for his nieces and nephews. He enjoys life to the fullest and spends time traveling and dating. In fact, he has been to every baseball stadium in the United States. He also owns his own home. John graduated from East Carolina University (which was the school he most desired to attend), majoring in Education. I was very excited he chose Education, knowing he would be an excellent teacher. He has worked in education for two decades while coaching the basketball team. He has coached gifted and talented students for several years, including those in the Odyssey of the Mind Program, leading those students on to state, regional, and national levels. Currently, he has returned to teach where he started school, the Cape Henlopen School District in Lewes, Delaware.

My second-born son, Jevon, and his wife are excellent parents. Their daughter, Jaylen, and son, Jace, are extremely intelligent. Jevon has been a federal agent for many years. His wife, Beth, has worked in high management positions throughout her career. They both unselfishly devote much time to the positive development of my grandchildren. Both Jaylen and Jace remain straight-A students and student-athletes in multiple sports. I am proud of all they have achieved, winning awards and trophies for both their academics and athletics. I hope they have learned from me that no matter how you start in life, you can rise above and become the best at whatever you wish to obtain.

Finally, my third son, Jerrin, being the youngest, outgrew his two brothers in every respect of life. He was the first to father five children, as well as the first to do many things before his brothers. Jerrin thought his greatest asset was being skillful with his hands. While part of this was true, Jerrin was a late bloomer, and I am proud of him for completing some college coursework. He surprised himself with how much he liked the program. He is currently only a few hours in coursework away from a nationally recognized certification in HVAC, heating, ventilation, and air conditioning.

As parents, we never know who we are raising.

Recently, I used something that I learned from a course entitled "Getting Ahead in a Just Getting by World" to save my mother's home. I then took that same information to help other people who were having home issues. One of those people was my sister, Brenda, whose home was at risk of being sold on her birthday on the steps of Fulton County Courthouse in Atlanta, Georgia. She passed away just a year prior. I did this simultaneously as I sold my uncle's home and helped him purchase another one, downsizing him after his wife's passing.

Even though all this had been taking place, I had to stay focused on completing my book. Even after becoming the caretaker of my mother and surviving the near-death experience at the hands of COVID, nothing was more important to me than to finish writing this book. And so I decided to relocate to the mountains in western Maryland and remain focused.

I am so grateful to the Denmark family and all the others in this area for accepting me graciously and helping me to achieve this goal. Thank you to First Missionary Baptist Church under the leadership of Pastor William Graham and his wonderful wife, who have been a welcoming substitute for me when I'm not able to be back to attend my church in Delaware. To Bishop Ralph R. Harmon and his wife, Ida, I offer many thanks for their leadership over my life. I'm full of gratitude. Anyone who has helped me in any way I wish to thank. Additionally, after a First Missionary Baptist Church change in leadership, Pastor Timothy McLaurin and his wife also accepted and welcomed me.

In addition, I would like to thank and express gratitude to BET for accepting my students every Saturday that I had the pleasure of driving to Washington, D.C., for them to have one of the best experiences of their lives, a live television appearance on Teen Summit.

I'd also like to thank Rachel Grier. I recently found out that she and I have so much in common. We strive to make the world a better place and to make sure that everyone is represented and treated well in life to the best of our abilities.

Down through the years, over a decade, each time I met Rachel, she would ask if I had completed my book. I'm so happy to say today, with Rachel's continuous encouragement, I have completed this goal. Rachel also provided me with a picture to put on the cover of my book, and I thank her for the beautiful artwork that now adorns the front.

I appreciate you, Rachel, for encouraging me to write this memoir.

# *Gratitude*

I express profound gratitude to the Denmark family for their unwavering support and kindness. I extend special recognition to Bishop Harmon of Faith, Hope and Love Christian Fellowship in Milford, DE, whose guidance has been invaluable. Appreciation is also extended to Rev. William Graham and his wife, Ida, from First Missionary Baptist Church for their inspiring leadership. My sincere thanks go to Rev. Timothy McLaurin and Leading Lady Kim McLaurin from First Missionary Baptist Church for their dedication and commitment. Furthermore, I appreciate BET Summit for providing a transformative television experience for our students every Saturday, enriching their lives in countless ways. Special appreciation to editors Ron Taylor, who started this journey assisting me, and Nicole Lockhart. Last but not least, I'm grateful for two role models who never knew me; however, I always admired them as they always inspired me: Maya Angelou and Oprah Winfrey.

## TO GOD BE THE GLORY

# *Affirmations/Inspirations*
## *A la Carte.*
## *—no charge*

## SELAH

"God doesn't always call the qualified
BUT God qualifies those he calls."

—Bishop TD Jakes

"When we rest, God cares;
when we care, God rests."

—Bishop Ralph R Harmon

"A day without laughter is a day wasted."

—Rev. William Graham

"The scars are our testimony."

—Rev. Timothy McLaurin

"God plus me is a Majority."

"He'll do it again."

—Song by Pastor Shirley Caesar

"Believe."

—Bishop Paul S. Morton

"Don't know what I'd do without the Lord."

—Grandpop Raymond Harmon

"Son, I thank God things are as well as they are."

—Grandmom Bessie

"Jesus is the center of my joy."

—Bishop R Harmon

"Don't borrow tomorrow's troubles;
they will take care of themselves."

—My mother, Elder Frances Hopkins

"God loves a cheerful, not careful, giver."

—My mother, Elder Frances Hopkins

"It's a long tide that never turns and a long road that never ends."

—My mother, Elder Frances Hopkins

"A closed hand can't give nor receive."

—My mother, Elder Frances Hopkins

"One can't be forgiven until one is forgiving."

—Barbara Wright

"TODAY is the TOMORROW
you worried about YESTERDAY."

—Pastor Timothy McLaurin

"I'm living my BLESSED life yet."

—Barbara Wright

"He knows my name."

—Tasha Cobbs

"Shifting the atmosphere."

—Jason Nelson

"FAITH is taking the first step even when
you don't see the entire staircase."

—Dr. Martin Luther King

ALWAYS walk into a room like God sent you.

TGIF—Thank God I Fought

ASAP—Always Say A Prayer.

# Photo Gallery

## FOUR GENERATIONS

**GRANDPOP**

**AUNT LYDIA AND UNCLE GEORGE**

**MaDear**

**BRENDA**

**MY MOTHER**

**MOM AND GRANDSON JOHN**

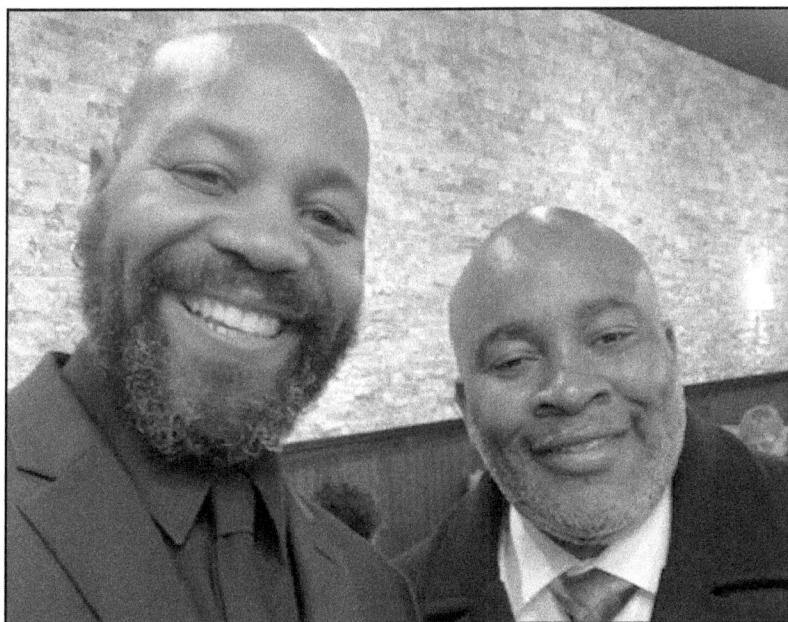

**ALVIN, BRENDA'S SON, AND MY SON JOHN**

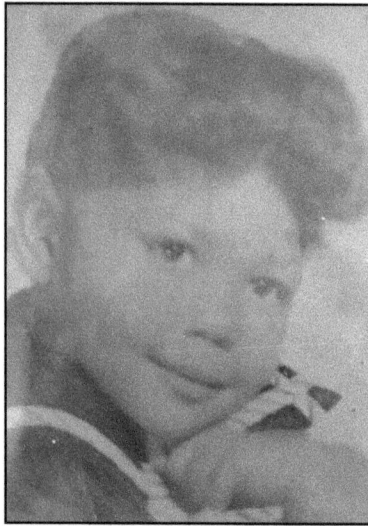

**MY EARLY PICTURE**

**MY HIGH SCHOOL PICTURE**

RESILIENT FORGIVENESS

## The Next Generation

**MY MOTHER AND HER GREAT-GRANDS**

**MY BROTHER COLEY**

RESILIENT FORGIVENESS

**JERMIA AND LAKHIRA**

**MY THREE SONS AT JEVON'S WEDDING**

**OLDER JERMIA GRADUATING FROM COLLEGE**

**JERMIA, CAMILA, AND KALI**